English for Listening, Speaking, Reading & Writing

NEW CONNECTION

BRING YOUR ENGLISH TO THE NEXT LEVEL

STUDENT BOOK 3

INTRODUCTION

Welcome to ***NEW CONNECTION*** — *BRING YOUR ENGLISH TO THE NEXT LEVEL.* This is the third book in a series created to propel learners toward fluency. Outstanding English skills will open up doors for anyone in today's world. No matter how out of reach a student's learning goals seem to be, the ***NEW CONNECTION*** series will provide the boost he or she needs.

Each unit of ***NEW CONNECTION*** — *BRING YOUR ENGLISH TO THE NEXT LEVEL* follows a set structure designed to push students to put what they have learned into practice as well as to challenge them to expand their skills. The unit begins with a **Words & Expressions** section, which utilizes both audio and visual methods to introduce words and expressions related to the topic. This is followed by a **Listen Up** exercise. At this time, learners will review vocabulary by answering questions based on a dialogue or monologue. The **Class Interview** section then gives learners a chance to put the vocabulary to use with a partner.

Students will move on to a video clip in which actors use new vocabulary — in addition to new grammar points and expressions — in real-life situations. They will listen along and fill in blanks too, and later be tested for comprehension. Afterwards, they're prompted to put freshly learned vocabulary and grammar skills to use in a series of review exercises. The unit ends with a related article and an opportunity for students to write their own compositions.

As students progress through each level, they are constantly encouraged to put what they have learned to use. At the same time, they never stop taking on new challenges to help themselves reach the next benchmark in the learning process. By developing a hunger for advancement, ***NEW CONNECTION*** — *BRING YOUR ENGLISH TO THE NEXT LEVEL* proves that the sky is the limit for today's learners.

CONTENTS

CONTENT CHART

Unit	Title	Subject	Conversation	Grammar
1	**Roommates**	Personality	The Perfect Person	Simple Future Tense
2	**Checking Out**	Shopping	Worldwide Bookstores	Adverbial Clauses
3	**Get in Shape**	Health	Lose Those Pounds	Noun Clauses
4	**Close Ties**	Relationships	The Breakup	Tag Questions
5	**Time to Celebrate**	Festivals	The Road to Mexico	Relative Clauses
6	**A Fine Art**	The Arts	Looking at Art	Factual and Unreal Conditionals
7	**Tune In**	Television	What to Watch?	Present Perfect Continuous
8	**Music to Our Ears**	Music	Two Tickets to the Concert	Types of Relative Clauses
9	**Study Abroad**	Study Abroad	A Big Decision	Adverbs
10	**Technology and You**	Technology	Making the Right Choice	Reported Speech
11	**Right and Wrong**	Morals	Caught on the Web	Subject and Verb Agreement
12	**Your Career Starts Now**	Careers	The Job Fair	Infinitives

	Reading	Writing
I Will I Be Going to I Present Continuous Tense I Common Time Expressions	Your Personality and Health	Roommate Ad
I Usage I Reduced Form	The Birth of eBay	Shopping Tips
I Form I Function I That Noun Clauses	Myths about Health and Exercise	Personal Trainer Ad
I Basic Structure I Special Cases	Dating around the World	Advice Column
I Relative Pronouns I Relative Pronoun Reduction I Prepositions in Relative Clauses	America's Unique Festivals	Festival Flyers
I Summary I Different Forms	The World's Most Uncommon Museums	Art Advice
I Form I Usage	The Unexpected Effects of Television	TV Habits
	The Healing Power of Music	Band Flyers
I Relative Adverbs I Conjunctive Adverbs	Adventures Abroad	Study Abroad Advice
I Requests / Orders I Questions I Statement	Robots Today and Tomorrow	Inventions
	College Students and Charity	Moral Advice
I Infinitives with Too and Enough I Infinitive Commands I Infinitives of Purpose	Work Cultures of the World	Job Applications

LEARNING OVERVIEW

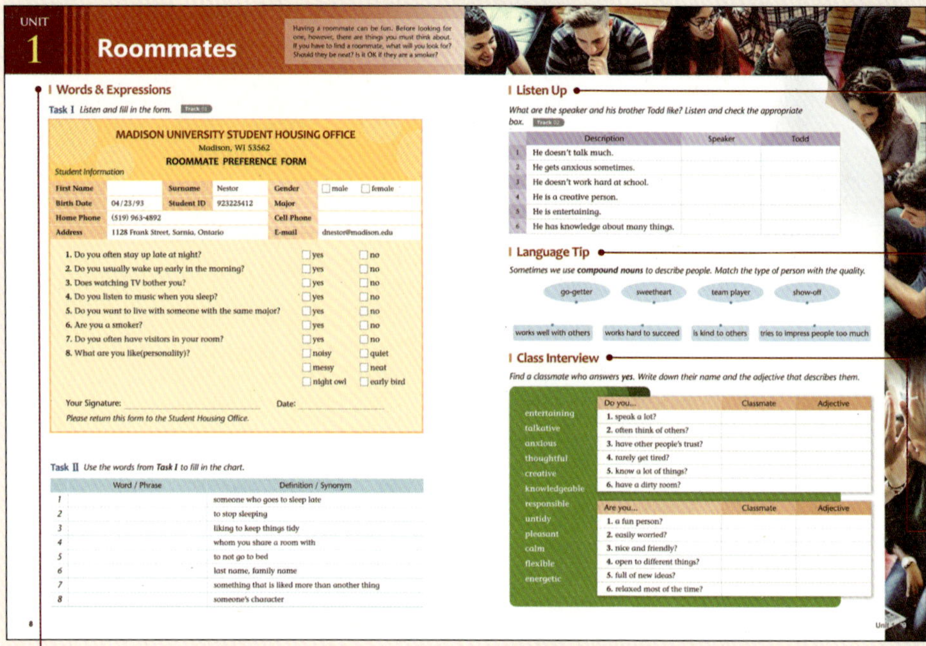

Listen Up

checks students' understanding of the words and expressions they have learned through listening comprehension questions.

Language Tip

helps students expand their vocabulary through various activities.

Class Interview

helps students understand the key expressions and words by practicing with a partner.

Words & Expressions

provides useful items with audio support to further students' understanding of the topic.

Conversation

includes a video clip helping students understand the content.

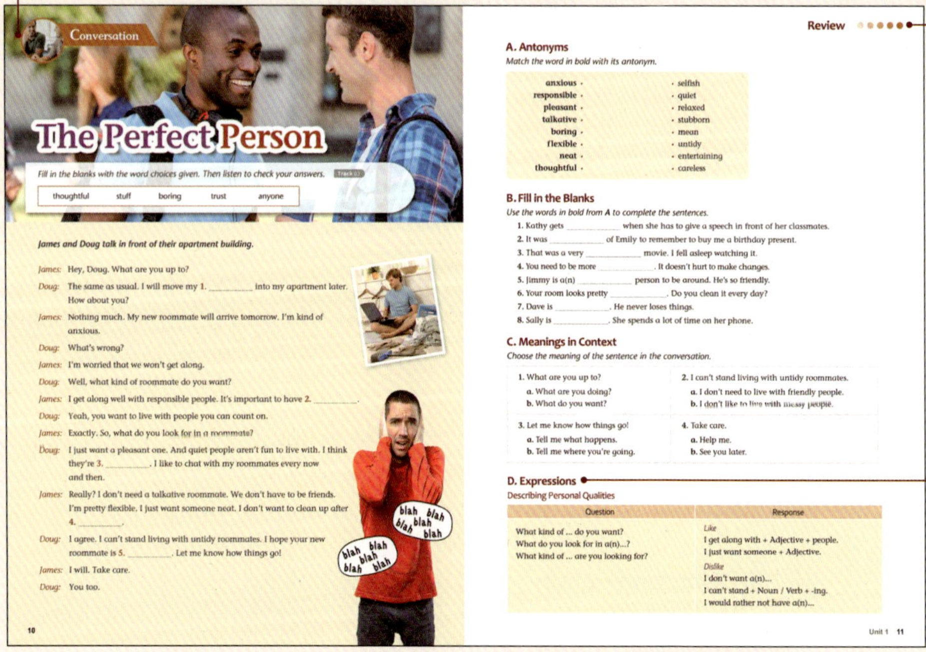

Review

checks students' understanding of the dialogue.

Expressions

provides everyday English usage and sentence structure.

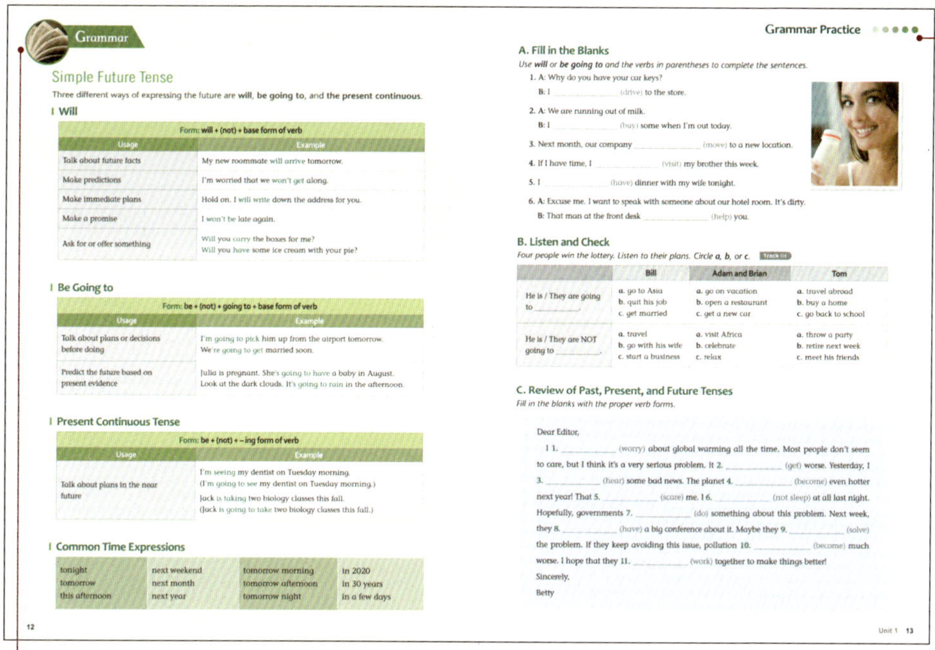

Grammar Practice

enables students to practice grammar in context to enhance accuracy and fluency.

Grammar

presents essential grammar to build overall accuracy.

Reading

enables students to broaden their knowledge through interesting articles.

After You Read

confirms students' understanding of the passage.

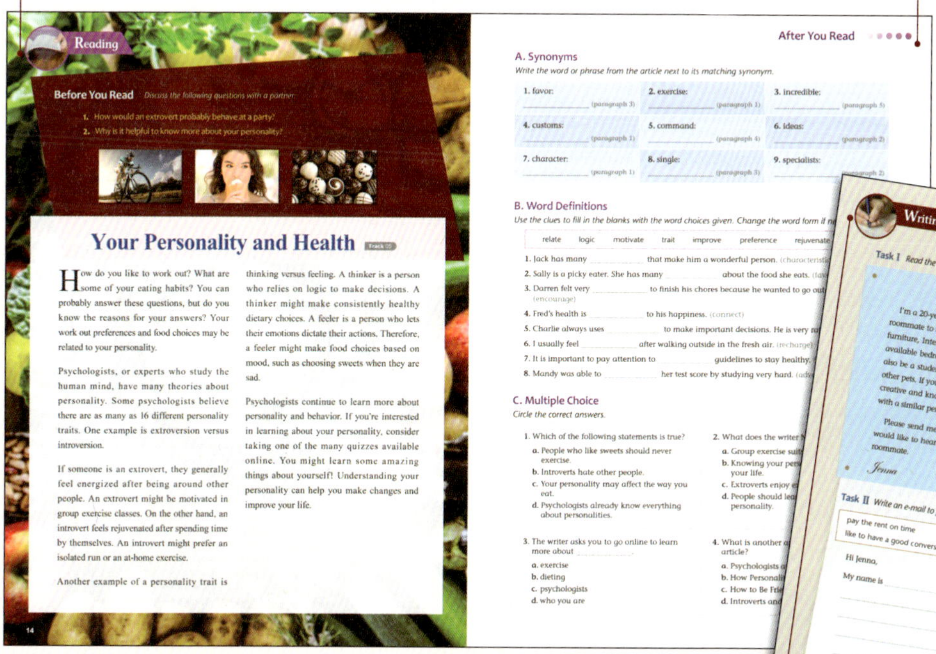

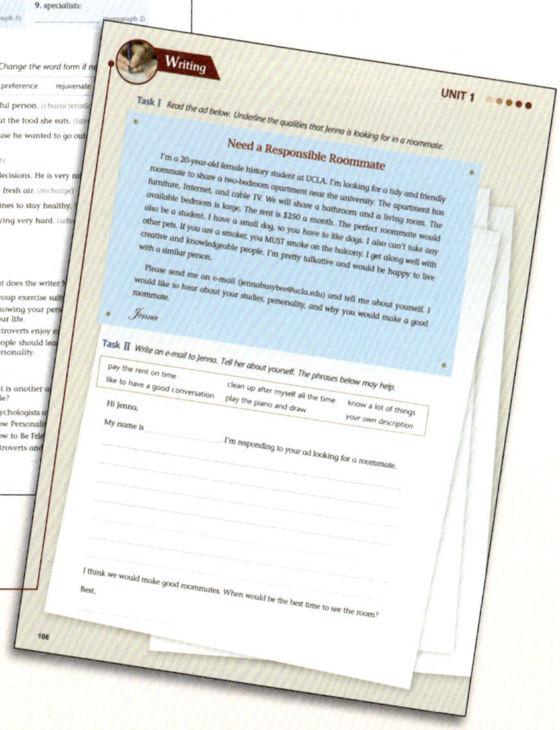

Writing

provides an opportunity for students to practice acquired language in authentic discourse using personalized content.

UNIT 1

Roommates

Having a roommate can be fun. Before looking one, however, there are things you must think ab If you have to find a roommate, what will you look Should they be neat? Is it OK if they are a smoker?

I Words & Expressions

Task I *Listen and fill in the form.* Track 01

MADISON UNIVERSITY STUDENT HOUSING OFFICE

Madison, WI 53562

ROOMMATE PREFERENCE FORM

Student Information

First Name		Surname	Nestor	Gender	☐ male ☐ female
Birth Date	04/23/93	Student ID	923225412	Major	
Home Phone	(519) 963-4892			Cell Phone	
Address	1128 Frank Street, Sarnia, Ontario			E-mail	dnestor@madison.edu

1. Do you often stay up late at night?	☐ yes	☐ no
2. Do you usually wake up early in the morning?	☐ yes	☐ no
3. Does watching TV bother you?	☐ yes	☐ no
4. Do you listen to music when you sleep?	☐ yes	☐ no
5. Do you want to live with someone with the same major?	☐ yes	☐ no
6. Are you a smoker?	☐ yes	☐ no
7. Do you often have visitors in your room?	☐ yes	☐ no
8. What are you like(personality)?	☐ noisy	☐ quiet
	☐ messy	☐ neat
	☐ night owl	☐ early bird

Your Signature: ______________________ Date: ______________

Please return this form to the Student Housing Office.

Task II *Use the words from* ***Task I*** *to fill in the chart.*

	Word / Phrase	Definition / Synonym
1		someone who goes to sleep late
2		to stop sleeping
3		liking to keep things tidy
4		whom you share a room with
5		to not go to bed
6		last name, family name
7		something that is liked more than another thing
8		someone's character

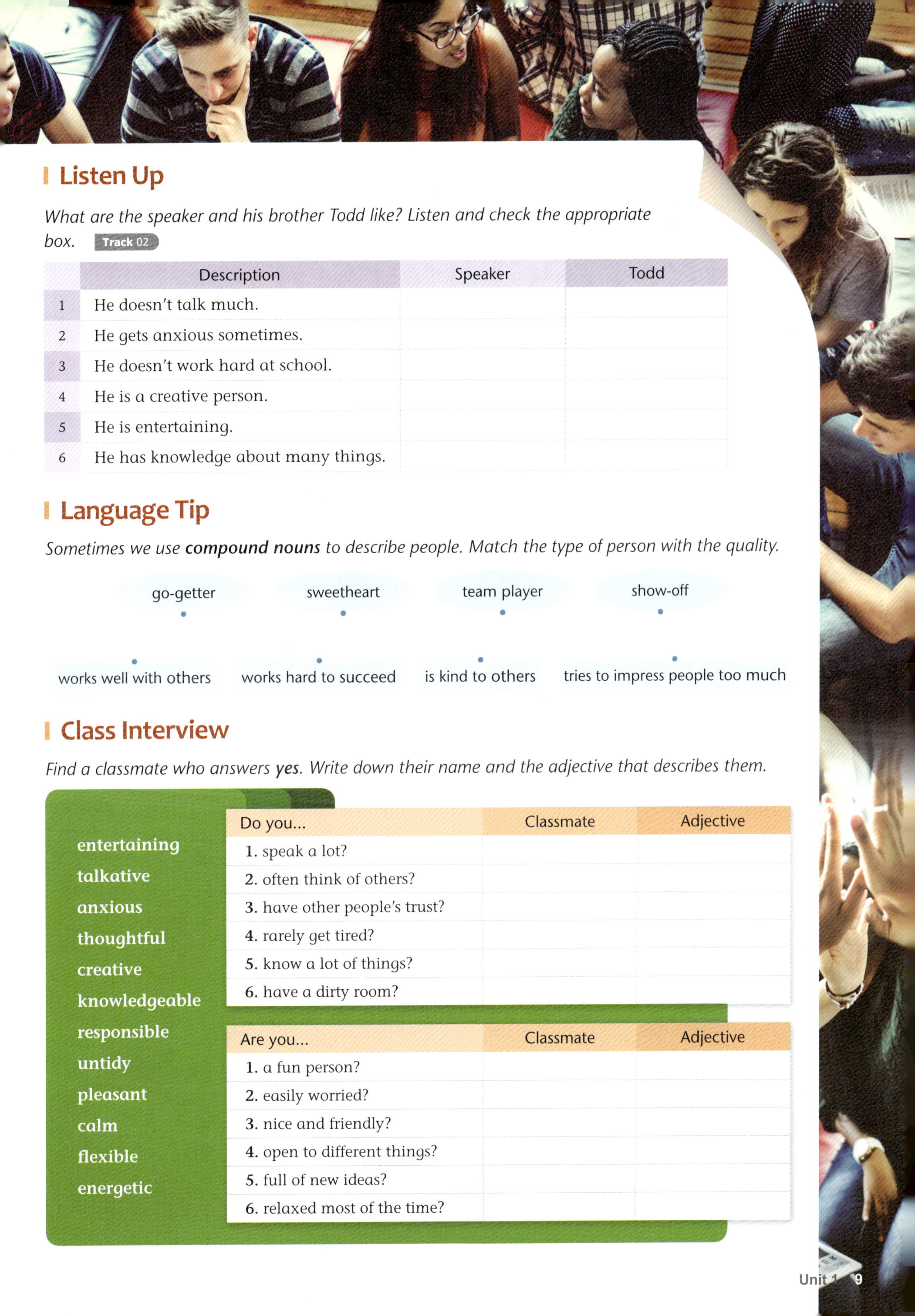

Listen Up

What are the speaker and his brother Todd like? Listen and check the appropriate box. Track 02

	Description	Speaker	Todd
1	He doesn't talk much.		
2	He gets anxious sometimes.		
3	He doesn't work hard at school.		
4	He is a creative person.		
5	He is entertaining.		
6	He has knowledge about many things.		

Language Tip

Sometimes we use ***compound nouns*** *to describe people. Match the type of person with the quality.*

go-getter • sweetheart • team player • show-off

works well with others • works hard to succeed • is kind to others • tries to impress people too much

Class Interview

Find a classmate who answers ***yes****. Write down their name and the adjective that describes them.*

entertaining
talkative
anxious
thoughtful
creative
knowledgeable
responsible
untidy
pleasant
calm
flexible
energetic

Do you...	Classmate	Adjective
1. speak a lot?		
2. often think of others?		
3. have other people's trust?		
4. rarely get tired?		
5. know a lot of things?		
6. have a dirty room?		

Are you...	Classmate	Adjective
1. a fun person?		
2. easily worried?		
3. nice and friendly?		
4. open to different things?		
5. full of new ideas?		
6. relaxed most of the time?		

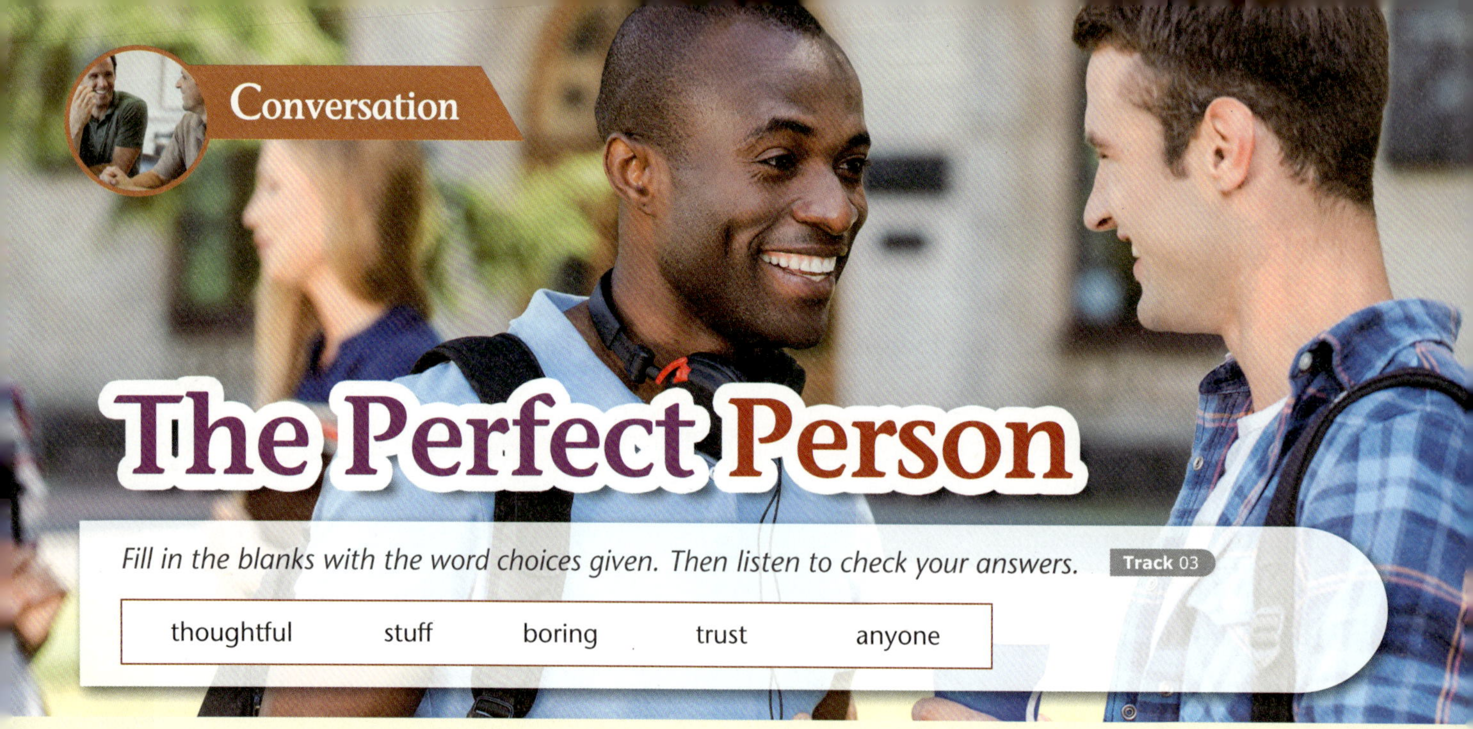

Conversation

The Perfect Person

Fill in the blanks with the word choices given. Then listen to check your answers. Track 03

thoughtful	stuff	boring	trust	anyone

James and Doug talk in front of their apartment building.

James: Hey, Doug. What are you up to?

Doug: The same as usual. I will move my **1.** __________ into my apartment later. How about you?

James: Nothing much. My new roommate will arrive tomorrow. I'm kind of anxious.

Doug: What's wrong?

James: I'm worried that we won't get along.

Doug: Well, what kind of roommate do you want?

James: I get along well with responsible people. It's important to have **2.** __________.

Doug: Yeah, you want to live with people you can count on.

James: Exactly. So, what do you look for in a roommate?

Doug: I just want a pleasant one. And quiet people aren't fun to live with. I think they're **3.** __________. I like to chat with my roommates every now and then.

James: Really? I don't need a talkative roommate. We don't have to be friends. I'm pretty flexible. I just want someone neat. I don't want to clean up after **4.** __________.

Doug: I agree. I can't stand living with untidy roommates. I hope your new roommate is **5.** __________. Let me know how things go!

James: I will. Take care.

Doug: You too.

A. Antonyms

Match the word in bold with its antonym.

anxious •	• selfish
responsible •	• quiet
pleasant •	• relaxed
talkative •	• stubborn
boring •	• mean
flexible •	• untidy
neat •	• entertaining
thoughtful •	• careless

B. Fill in the Blanks

*Use the words in bold from **A** to complete the sentences.*

1. Kathy gets ______________ when she has to give a speech in front of her classmates.
2. It was ______________ of Emily to remember to buy me a birthday present.
3. That was a very ______________ movie. I fell asleep watching it.
4. You need to be more ______________. It doesn't hurt to make changes.
5. Jimmy is a(n) ______________ person to be around. He's so friendly.
6. Your room looks pretty ______________. Do you clean it every day?
7. Dave is ______________. He never loses things.
8. Sally is ______________. She spends a lot of time on her phone.

C. Meanings in Context

Choose the meaning of the sentence in the conversation.

1. What are you up to?
- **a.** What are you doing?
- **b.** What do you want?

2. I can't stand living with untidy roommates.
- **a.** I don't need to live with friendly people.
- **b.** I don't like to live with messy people.

3. Let me know how things go!
- **a.** Tell me what happens.
- **b.** Tell me where you're going.

4. Take care.
- **a.** Help me.
- **b.** See you later.

D. Expressions

Describing Personal Qualities

Question	Response
What kind of ... do you want? What do you look for in a(n)...? What kind of ... are you looking for?	*Like* I get along with + Adjective + people. I just want someone + Adjective. *Dislike* I don't want a(n)... I can't stand + Noun / Verb + -ing. I would rather not have a(n)...

Grammar

Simple Future Tense

Three different ways of expressing the future are **will**, **be going to**, and **the present continuous**.

Will

Form: will + (not) + base form of verb	
Usage	**Example**
Talk about future facts	My new roommate will arrive tomorrow.
Make predictions	I'm worried that we won't get along.
Make immediate plans	Hold on. I will write down the address for you.
Make a promise	I won't be late again.
Ask for or offer something	Will you carry the boxes for me? Will you have some ice cream with your pie?

Be Going to

Form: be + (not) + going to + base form of verb	
Usage	**Example**
Talk about plans or decisions before doing	I'm going to pick him up from the airport tomorrow. We're going to get married soon.
Predict the future based on present evidence	Julia is pregnant. She's going to have a baby in August. Look at the dark clouds. It's going to rain in the afternoon.

Present Continuous Tense

Form: be + (not) + – ing form of verb	
Usage	**Example**
Talk about plans in the near future	I'm seeing my dentist on Tuesday morning. (I'm going to see my dentist on Tuesday morning.) Jack is taking two biology classes this fall. (Jack is going to take two biology classes this fall.)

Common Time Expressions

tonight	next weekend	tomorrow morning	in 2020
tomorrow	next month	tomorrow afternoon	in 30 years
this afternoon	next year	tomorrow night	in a few days

A. Fill in the Blanks

*Use **will** or **be going to** and the verbs in parentheses to complete the sentences.*

1. A: Why do you have your car keys?
   B: I ________________ (drive) to the store.

2. A: We are running out of milk.
   B: I ________________ (buy) some when I'm out today.

3. Next month, our company ________________ (move) to a new location.

4. If I have time, I ________________ (visit) my brother this week.

5. I ________________ (have) dinner with my wife tonight.

6. A: Excuse me. I want to speak with someone about our hotel room. It's dirty.
   B: That man at the front desk ________________ (help) you.

B. Listen and Check

*Four people win the lottery. Listen to their plans. Circle **a**, **b**, or **c**.* Track 04

	Bill	Adam and Brian	Tom
He is / They are going to ___________.	a. go to Asia b. quit his job c. get married	a. go on vacation b. open a restaurant c. get a new car	a. travel abroad b. buy a home c. go back to school
He is / They are NOT going to ___________.	a. travel b. go with his wife c. start a business	a. visit Africa b. celebrate c. relax	a. throw a party b. retire next week c. meet his friends

C. Review of Past, Present, and Future Tenses

Fill in the blanks with the proper verb forms.

Dear Editor,

I **1.** ______________ (worry) about global warming all the time. Most people don't seem to care, but I think it's a very serious problem. It **2.** ______________ (get) worse. Yesterday, I **3.** ______________ (hear) some bad news. The planet **4.** ______________ (become) even hotter next year! That **5.** ______________ (scare) me. I **6.** ______________ (not sleep) at all last night. Hopefully, governments **7.** ______________ (do) something about this problem. Next week, they **8.** ______________ (have) a big conference about it. Maybe they **9.** ______________ (solve) the problem. If they keep avoiding this issue, pollution **10.** ______________ (become) much worse. I hope that they **11.** ______________ (work) together to make things better!

Sincerely,

Betty

Reading

Before You Read *Discuss the following questions with a partner:*

1. How would an extrovert probably behave at a party?
2. Why is it helpful to know more about your personality?

Your Personality and Health

Track 05

How do you like to work out? What are some of your eating habits? You can probably answer these questions, but do you know the reasons for your answers? Your work out preferences and food choices may be related to your personality.

Psychologists, or experts who study the human mind, have many theories about personality. Some psychologists believe there are as many as 16 different personality traits. One example is extroversion versus introversion.

If someone is an extrovert, they generally feel energized after being around other people. An extrovert might be motivated in group exercise classes. On the other hand, an introvert feels rejuvenated after spending time by themselves. An introvert might prefer an isolated run or an at-home exercise.

Another example of a personality trait is thinking versus feeling. A thinker is a person who relies on logic to make decisions. A thinker might make consistently healthy dietary choices. A feeler is a person who lets their emotions dictate their actions. Therefore, a feeler might make food choices based on mood, such as choosing sweets when they are sad.

Psychologists continue to learn more about personality and behavior. If you're interested in learning about your personality, consider taking one of the many quizzes available online. You might learn some amazing things about yourself! Understanding your personality can help you make changes and improve your life.

A. Synonyms

Write the word or phrase from the article next to its matching synonym.

1. favor: ______________ (paragraph 3)	2. exercise: ______________ (paragraph 1)	3. incredible: ______________ (paragraph 5)
4. customs: ______________ (paragraph 1)	5. command: ______________ (paragraph 4)	6. ideas: ______________ (paragraph 2)
7. character: ______________ (paragraph 1)	8. single: ______________ (paragraph 3)	9. specialists: ______________ (paragraph 2)

B. Word Definitions

Use the clues to fill in the blanks with the word choices given. Change the word form if necessary.

relate	logic	motivate	trait	improve	preference	rejuvenate	dietary

1. Jack has many ______________ that make him a wonderful person. (characteristic)
2. Sally is a picky eater. She has many ______________ about the food she eats. (favorite)
3. Darren felt very ______________ to finish his chores because he wanted to go out with his friends. (encourage)
4. Fred's health is ______________ to his happiness. (connect)
5. Charlie always uses ______________ to make important decisions. He is very rational. (reason)
6. I usually feel ______________ after walking outside in the fresh air. (recharge)
7. It is important to pay attention to ______________ guidelines to stay healthy. (nutritional)
8. Mandy was able to ______________ her test score by studying very hard. (advance)

C. Multiple Choice

Circle the correct answers.

1. Which of the following statements is true?
   a. People who like sweets should never exercise.
   b. Introverts hate other people.
   c. Your personality may affect the way you eat.
   d. Psychologists already know everything about personalities.

2. What does the writer NOT agree with?
   a. Group exercise suits introverts.
   b. Knowing your personality can improve your life.
   c. Extroverts enjoy exercising in groups.
   d. People should learn about their personality.

3. The writer asks you to go online to learn more about ______________.
   a. exercise
   b. dieting
   c. psychologists
   d. who you are

4. What is another appropriate title for the article?
   a. Psychologists and Other Experts
   b. How Personality Affects Health
   c. How to Be Friends with Everyone
   d. Introverts and Extroverts

UNIT 2

Checking Out

These days, people are able to buy things directly f websites. Of course, some people still prefer tc shopping the old way — in stores. How about you you ever do your shopping on the Internet?

I Words & Expressions

Task I *Listen to the two dialogues. Check the advertisement that matches each dialogue.* Track 06

☐ 

☐ 

☐ 

☐ 

Task II *Use the words from **Task I** to fill in the chart.*

	Word / Phrase	Definition
1		something you buy at a good price
2		a cut in the usual price
3		things to choose from
4		every year
5		when a store sells things at a lower price
6		how a customer may give back a product
7		the name of a company
8		sending products to the buyer

Listen Up

Eric has recently bought a TV online. Check the statements he would likely agree with. Track 07

- ☐ He had to pay for delivery.
- ☐ TVs online were more expensive than those in the stores.
- ☐ Eric likes to see the salesperson when he buys something.
- ☐ There were a lot of different televisions available on the Internet.
- ☐ The television was broken when it got to his house.

Language Tip

When you get a **discount**, you pay less than the usual price. A **bargain** is a product that you get a good deal on.

Fill in the blanks with the appropriate words.

1. Hotel guests get a 15 percent ______________ at the gym.
2. This rice cooker is a better ______________ than that one. It costs half the price.
3. At $25, this jacket is a real ______________!

Class Interview

Ask your classmates about shopping.

1. What time of the year do you find the best bargains?
2. How much time do you spend shopping each week?
3. What's the best thing about shopping in person?

Write down their opinions about online shopping. The words below may help.

convenient	product	safe	delivery	selection
price	time-saving	impersonal	bargain	compare

Online Shopping			
Good		Bad	
Opinion	Classmate	Opinion	Classmate
1. It's really convenient to shop from home.		1. I prefer to see the product with my own eyes.	
2.		2.	
3.		3.	
4.		4.	

Conversation

Worldwide Bookstores

Fill in the blanks with the word choices given. Then listen to check your answers. Track 08

type in	bargains	print	additional	discount	online

James runs into Shelly at a bookstore.

James: How's it going, Shelly? Book shopping?

Shelly: Hi, James. I'm having some trouble finding a book.

James: Why not try **1.** __________?

Shelly: I've never bought anything online before.

James: You should give it a shot. You can get great **2.** __________, and there's a big selection.

Shelly: I don't have a clue where to start.

James: No problem! I'll help you.

Shelly: Great. Thanks, James.

(Back at home, Shelly is sitting at the computer.)

James: First, you need to **3.** __________ the book's name.

Shelly: OK. I see it. The price looks pretty good.

James: If you want to buy it, you can click there. Make sure you read the whole page because there could be **4.** __________ charges.

Shelly: Ah. I see. There's a huge delivery fee, and it will be a whole month before it arrives.

James: Always pay attention to the small **5.** __________. Hopefully, you can find it on another site.

(Shelly types.)

Shelly: What do you think about this one?

James: It looks amazing! There's a 20 percent **6.** __________.
You see? While it seems difficult at first, it's actually quite easy.

Shelly: Hmm. I'm uncertain about giving my credit card details. I don't trust websites.

James: You should be careful when buying online, but this site has gotten excellent reviews.

A. Word Definitions

Use the clues to fill in the blanks with the word choices given.

worldwide	run into	additional	fee
pay attention to	hopefully	amazing	discount

1. If you're buying a laptop, it's a good idea to buy a(n) ______________ battery. (extra)
2. We were successful last time, so ______________ it will be the same this time. (you wish)
3. You can get a(n) ______________ on most items if you have a loyalty card. (reduced price)
4. Our company has a(n) ______________ delivery service. (international)
5. I often ______________ Karen when she's shopping in the city. (meet by accident)
6. You should ______________ your handwriting. People can't read it. (be careful with)
7. Have you tried the ______________ new Italian restaurant down the street? (great)
8. We can arrange airport pickup for a small ______________. (charge)

B. Meanings in Context

Choose the meaning of the sentence in the conversation.

1. You should give it a shot.
   a. It's a good idea to try it.
   b. Why not take a picture?

2. I don't have a clue where to start.
   a. I don't have the tools to start work.
   b. I don't know how to begin.

3. The price looks pretty good.
   a. The item seems like a bargain.
   b. The product is beautiful.

4. I'm uncertain about giving my credit card details.
   a. I don't know if I should give my details.
   b. I feel very bad about giving my details.

5. This site has gotten excellent reviews.
   a. People have looked at this site again and again.
   b. People have said good things about the site.

C. Expressions

Making Suggestions

Informal	Standard	Formal	More Polite
Why not + Verb ...? Why don't you + Verb ...? How about + Verb + -ing ...? What about + Verb + -ing ...? Let's + Verb ...	You should ... You'd better + Verb ... You can ...	I suggest (that) you (should) + Verb ... I advise you to + Verb ...	You could always ... Perhaps you could ... It might be a good idea to ...

Use the expressions above to change the following. Practice saying the suggestions to a partner.

1. Why not take a few days off and go on vacation?
2. How about going jogging before breakfast?
3. What about looking for a new job?

Grammar

Adverbial Clauses

Usage

Adverbial clauses are used as an adverb in a sentence. They must be connected to an independent clause.

Type	Example
Time	It will be a whole month before it arrives. I will give you a call when I get home. You should shut off your computer after you finish work.
Cause and effect	Make sure you read the whole page because there could be extra charges. Since we don't know the answer, we should ask the teacher for help.
Contrast	While it seems difficult at first, it's actually quite easy. Although he doesn't like books, Mark works in a library.
Condition	If you want to buy it, you can click there. Milk quickly turns sour unless you put it in the refrigerator.

Usage Note

While often means **when**. It can also be used to show a difference between two things.

For Example:

While Larry was watching TV this morning, he saw a mouse on the carpet. (when)
While Tomas can speak French, I cannot. (difference)

Reduced Form

When the subject of the adverbial clause and the subject of the main clause are the same, we can reduce the adverbial clause to make the sentence shorter.

Full Adverbial Clause	Reduced Adverbial Clause
You should be careful when you buy online.	You should be careful when buying online.
While I was skating last night, I fell down and cut my leg.	While skating last night, I fell down and cut my leg.
After he finished the report, Jay sent it to the manager.	After finishing the report, Jay sent it to the manager.
Because she wanted to exercise more, Karen went to the gym every day.	Wanting to exercise more, Karen went to the gym every day.

A. Combine the Sentences

Connect the sentences using the words given.

1. You don't want to eat out. / Let's cook something here. (since)

   → ______________________________

2. Their team hasn't won a single game this year. / Ours has won six. (while)

   → ______________________________

3. I want to travel the world. / I'm too old. (before)

   → ______________________________

4. You want to play the violin well. / You have to practice. (if)

   → ______________________________

5. There weren't any books in the waiting room. / Jeff read a magazine instead. (because)

   → ______________________________

B. Reduce Adverbial Clauses

Fill in the blanks with the reduced forms. Put an X if it's impossible to reduce the clause.

1. I went to the park **after** I ate lunch.

   → I went to the park ______________ lunch.

2. **Because** I was late for dinner, most of the food was gone.

   → ______________ for dinner, most of the food was gone.

3. **Before** he wrote his book, Derek traveled to Africa to do research.

   → ______________ his book, Derek traveled to Africa to do research.

4. Amy kept asking me questions **while** I was doing my homework.

   → Amy kept asking me questions ______________ my homework.

5. **Although** he felt afraid, Jeffrey tried hard to remain calm.

   → ______________ afraid, Jeffrey tried hard to remain calm.

C. Correct the Mistakes

Fix the errors in the passage.

Encyclopedias have been around for a long time. In 77 AD, an encyclopedia of natural history, *Naturalis Historia*, was published by a Roman, Pliny the Elder. This book was both written and copied by hand. Now we can publish things quickly. In Hawaiian, the word for quick is "wiki." After ~~be~~ being put online, Wikipedia has been used by millions of people. Because it is an open encyclopedia, so anyone can edit it. While it introducing lots of topics, people question the information. The problem is that the writers are not experts. However, there are a lot of them. One person gets it wrong, another can correct it. After ten years, Wikipedia is still free and still going strong. Although isn't perfect, it's a useful tool.

Reading

Before You Read *Discuss the following questions with a partner:*

1. Where do you usually do your shopping?
2. Do you remember the first time you purchased an item online?

The Birth of eBay

Track 09

eBay is the biggest shopping website in the world and it makes billions of dollars each year. Thousands of objects are sold and purchased on eBay every day, including items as expensive as fighter jets and houses. However, eBay had very humble beginnings.

eBay was founded in 1995 by Pierre Omidyar. It began when he listed his broken laser pointer for sale online as an experiment. He was surprised when someone offered to purchase it for $14.83. Omidyar sent an e-mail to the buyer in order to remind him that the laser pointer was damaged. The purchaser responded by saying, "I collect broken laser pointers." Realizing the Internet was full of opportunities like this, Omidyar created AuctionWeb. AuctionWeb was an online marketplace where sellers could list items for sale in an auction format. On its first day, the site did not attract any visits. However, within a year, AuctionWeb started to make a profit. Soon, Omidyar was even able to quit his day job. In 1997, AuctionWeb's name was officially changed to eBay.

In the years since then, eBay has been so successful that it has even managed to buy other popular Internet companies, such as Skype and Craigslist. Today, eBay continues to connect millions of buyers and sellers online.

A. Synonyms

Write the word or phrase from the article next to its matching synonym.

1. chances: ______ (paragraph 2)	**2.** buy: ______ (paragraph 2)	**3.** succeeded in (doing): ______ (paragraph 3)
4. currently: ______ (paragraph 3)	**5.** established: ______ (paragraph 2)	**6.** replied: ______ (paragraph 2)
7. costly: ______ (paragraph 1)	**8.** earn money: ______ (paragraph 2)	**9.** damaged: ______ (paragraph 2)

B. Words with Different Meanings

Match the word in bold with its definition.

1. Our home is quite **humble**. It only has two bedrooms. ______
   He is modest and **humble**. He never brags about his accomplishments. ______
   Definition: ⓐ *adj.* not proud ⓑ *adj.* not big or expensive

2. Jerry decided to **change** his career and become a firefighter. ______
   Hannah counted the **change** she received from the cashier. ______
   Definition: ⓐ *n.* coins ⓑ *v.* to modify or switch something

3. Mr. Willis is going to **manage** the baseball team. ______
   The test was not easy, but I **managed** to pass it. ______
   Definition: ⓐ *v.* to try hard and finish something difficult ⓑ *v.* to direct or control

C. Put in Order

Put the statements in order from 1 – 5.

______ A bidder bought the broken laser pointer online for the price of $14.83.
______ eBay purchased the online companies Skype and Craigslist.
______ Pierre Omidyar stopped working at his day job.
______ The website AuctionWeb was not successful in the beginning.
______ AuctionWeb officially became eBay.

D. True or False

*Check **True** or **False**.*

	True	False
1. Pierre Omidyar is the founder of eBay.	☐	☐
2. Pierre Omidyar knew he'd be able to sell the laser pointer for $14.83.	☐	☐
3. eBay cost billions of dollars to set up.	☐	☐
4. AuctionWeb did not make any money until five years after it began.	☐	☐
5. eBay has expanded by purchasing other online companies.	☐	☐

UNIT 3

Get in Shape

Is it difficult to get up in the morning? Do you sometimes fall asleep in class? Exercising can help you stay energetic throughout the day.

I Words & Expressions

Task I *Listen to Jessica talking about her health. Fill in the blanks and check the boxes.* Track 10

GENERAL INFORMATION	1. How tall is Jessica? ________ cm 2. What is her current weight? ________ kg 3. What is her waist size? ________ cm
FEELINGS	4. Recently, Jessica has ... □ not been able to concentrate on her studies. □ had things to motivate her. □ been under a lot of pressure. □ had trouble dealing with her problems. □ experienced depression.
DIET	5. On average, how many portions of fruit and vegetables does she eat a day? □ four to five □ a couple □ none 6. How often does she eat fast food? □ seldom □ once a month □ daily 7. How much alcohol does she drink? □ She doesn't drink. □ more than three glasses a day □ a couple of glasses a week
PHYSICAL ACTIVITY	8. How often does she work out? □ every day, for an hour or more □ never □ three times a week, for at least 30 minutes

Task II *Use the words given to complete the sentences.*

concentrate on	motivate	pressure	depression
on average	portion	daily	physical

1. Could you please turn down the TV? I need to ____________ my homework.
2. People watch 28 hours of television every week ____________.
3. Emma is very healthy because she jogs ____________.
4. A big part of being a teacher is to ____________ students.
5. Teenagers are under a lot of ____________ to pass exams.
6. I like to play ____________ sports, like boxing and hockey.
7. John was hungry, so he ordered a bigger ____________.
8. Women experience ____________ nearly twice as often as men.

Listen Up

*Listen and check **True** or **False**.* Track 11

	True	False
1. Her mother says she should eat healthy food.	☐	☐
2. Her mother is a gym teacher.	☐	☐
3. Her father thinks that working out is important for staying healthy.	☐	☐
4. She likes to take part in athletic events.	☐	☐
5. When eating, she eats big portions.	☐	☐
6. Eating a lot of food helps to keep her awake in class.	☐	☐

Language Tip

When someone is healthy, we'll often say they're **in shape**. To describe someone's body, we'll usually use **figure** (for women) and **build** (for men).

Fill in the blanks with the appropriate words.

1. Wow! The actress in this movie has a great ______________.
2. I hired a personal trainer to help me get back ______________.
3. My brother has a strong ______________. He wants to become a professional football player.

Class Interview

Look at the quotes below. Who are the people? What do they do?

Michael Jordan: Conditioning and nutrition are important to participating in athletic events.
Patrick Dempsey: I need to be in shape to be competitive as a racecar driver.
Aaron Eckhart: Even after a late night, I get up and run at six a.m. It keeps me alert.
Michelle Obama: We can make portion sizes smaller and emphasize quality over quantity.

Write the names of the famous people and your own tip. Ask a partner which is most important.

How Do They Stay Healthy?	Most Important
1. ______________ recommends small amounts of food.	
2. Jogging can help wake up ______________.	
3. ______________ trained and ate right to compete.	
4. ______________ needs to be fit to be good at his job. (Your own tip)	

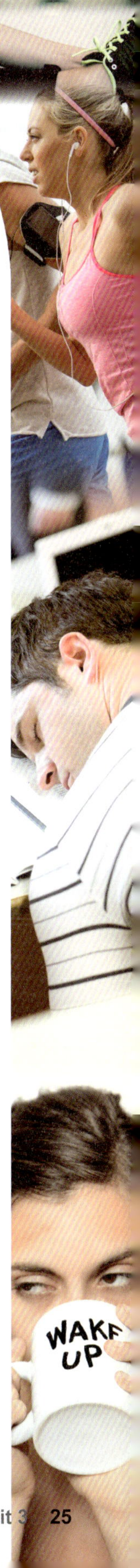

Conversation

Lose Those Pounds

Fill in the blanks with the word choices given. Then listen to check your answers. Track 12

accompany	weight	motivation	tight	faint

Darla meets James outside the campus restaurant.

Darla: I'm really packing on the pounds.

James: What? You're in good shape, Darla.

Darla: I can't fit into my favorite dress. It's too **1.** __________.

James: How about going on a diet then? You can change your **2.** __________ by what you eat.

Darla: I am on a diet. I eat 1,250 calories a day on average. The portions are really small. I'm so weak that I can't move. Every time I try to stand up, I feel like I'm going to **3.** __________.

James: That sounds awful. What I suggest is following a different diet. It should be high in protein and low in fat, with plenty of whole grains too.

Darla: I'm trying to lose weight, so I can't eat a lot of food.

James: You can't stand up though. How will you exercise?

Darla: I don't think that I want to exercise. I hate sports.

James: Your problem is that you need some **4.** __________.
Why not run in the park or go swimming?

Darla: I don't feel up to running, but I'm willing to go swimming if you'll **5.** __________ me. You can help motivate me.

James: It's a deal.

A. Meanings in Context

Choose the meaning of the sentence in the conversation.

1. I'm really packing on the pounds.
a. I'm getting fatter.
b. I'm getting thinner.

2. You're in good shape, Darla.
a. You look fit.
b. You're good at making shapes.

3. I am on a diet.
a. I eat different kinds of food.
b. I control what I eat.

4. I don't feel up to running.
a. I don't feel well enough to run.
b. I don't like running uphill.

5. You can help motivate me.
a. You can teach me how to exercise.
b. If you are there, it will encourage me.

B. Words with Different Meanings

Match the word in bold with its definition.

1
He's getting big. He doesn't **fit** into the baby seat anymore. ______
He **fits** in well with the other students. ______
The pants **fit** her very nicely. ______
Definition: ⓐ *v.* to become part of the group ⓑ *v.* to get into ⓒ *v.* to be the right size

2
This shirt is so **tight** that I can't lift my arms. ______
He held on **tight** to the chair during the earthquake. ______
Definition: ⓐ *adj.* too small ⓑ *adv.* very firmly

3
I feel **faint** because I've been in the sun for too long. ______
He was so afraid that he **fainted** onto the floor. ______
Definition: ⓐ *adj.* feeling weak and unwell ⓑ *v.* to fall over as if asleep

C. Expressions

Talking about Diets

Very Little	low in	fat salt
Lots of	high in rich in full of	protein sugar calcium

Usage Note

We also use compound adjectives to talk about diets.

For Example:
Eggs are a **high-protein** food. (Eggs are **high in protein**.)

Rewrite the sentences using the expressions above.

1. Kids like foods with lots of sugar.
→ Kids' snacks are usually ______________________.
2. She has heart problems, so she has to eat less salt.
→ As she has heart problems, her diet has to be ______________________.

Grammar

Noun Clauses

A noun clause is a group of words with a subject and verb. A noun clause cannot be by itself as a sentence.

Form

Wh– word + Subject + Verb	who the man is, whatever you like
Whether / if + Subject + Verb	whether it rains, if she will remember me
Wh– word + to Verb	when to meet, what to say
That + Subject + Verb	that I like, that she wants

Function

A subject of a verb	What I suggest is following a different diet.
An object of a verb	I don't think that I want to exercise.
A subject complement	Your problem is that you need some motivation.
An object of a preposition	You can change your weight by what you eat.
An adjective complement	Everyone is glad that Betty is getting married.

That Noun Clauses

That noun clauses usually follow ...

Subject + Verb	agree, believe, decide, guess, hope, think, suggest, recommend ...
I agree that we need more teachers for the school.	
Subject + be + Adjective	afraid, angry, glad, worried, sorry, sure, surprised ...
Tommy was surprised that you didn't invite him to your wedding.	
It + be + Adjective	amazing, clear, good, important, necessary, possible, true ...
It is possible that we'll have to take the exam in February.	

Usage Note

Some adjectives and verbs require the base verb form.

For Example:

It is **important** that you leave now.
The doctor **recommends** that the patient quit smoking.

A. Rewrite the Sentences

*Complete the sentences using a **noun clause**.*

1. Whom did you talk to earlier?
   → Jean asked me ______________________________.
2. Where did Mike learn how to skate?
   → I wonder ______________________________.
3. How did he get the job?
   → ______________________________ is a mystery.
4. We don't communicate well.
   → Our problem is ______________________________.
5. Why is that woman standing outside?
   → He is curious about ______________________________.
6. We need to take out the trash tomorrow.
   → It is important ______________________________.

B. Multiple Choice

Circle the answers.

1. I lost my mother's ring. She asked me where __________.
   a. is her ring b. her ring was c. is your ring d. was her ring
2. The neighbors are playing their music loudly. I can't hear what __________.
   a. is saying you b. you says c. you are saying d. that you says
3. The little boy next door is popular, but I don't know how many __________.
   a. friends does he have b. does he have friends
   c. friends has he d. friends he has
4. I'm not going to fix up my apartment. __________ is too expensive.
   a. Whether I want to do b. What do I want to do
   c. What I want to do d. That I want to do

C. Match

Match the two parts.

1.	Can you tell me what	she return to the hospital tomorrow.
2.	Do you know where	I didn't pass the exam.
3.	I'm worried that	the nearest post office is?
4.	The doctor suggested that	I can't come to your party.
5.	I'm sorry that	I should eat when I'm on a low-fat diet?
6.	What he gave Anna	we'll all be friends.
7.	Did you hear about	meant a lot to her.
8.	My hope is that	what they did?

Reading

Before You Read *Discuss the following questions with a partner:*

1. Which foods are rich in protein?
2. What should you do before starting a new diet or exercise plan?

Myths about Health and Exercise

Track 13

Nutritionists, researchers, and even personal trainers seem to have varying opinions about which foods constitute a healthy diet. Likewise, there have been many fitness trends throughout the years. However, did you know that there are several popular myths about diet and exercise? Unfortunately, if you do not discover the truth about these myths, your health routine could be less effective.

One widely-believed myth is that consuming a late-night meal will lead to greater weight gain as opposed to an earlier dinner. The popular thought is that your body will not be able to burn the calories that you consumed right before bed and instead convert them into fat. However, today's experts agree that the time of day that you consume calories should not be your focus. Instead you should pay attention to how many total calories you ingest. The reason for this is that any excess calories will be turned into fat, regardless of when they are consumed.

Another common misguided notion involves the popularity of diet sodas. The average person believes that diet sodas are a healthy option, compared to regular sodas, since diet drinks have no calories. However, considering these drinks "healthy" is faulty thinking. Some studies have linked drinking diet soda to certain diseases, such as diabetes, since diet drinks contain artificial sweeteners.

Weight lifters are known for having protein-rich diets, but many people believe the myth that vegetarians struggle to build muscle since their diet lacks protein. This is incorrect thinking as well. Protein can be found in foods other than meat, such as beans, nuts, and grains.

Rather than following common thinking, you can improve your health routine by researching today's scientific findings. Understanding the truth about common myths will help you to make healthier choices.

A. Words with Different Meanings

Match the word in bold with its definition.

1 Nothing special happened today. It was just another **routine** day. ______

When I get to work, I follow the same **routine**. I turn on the computer and make coffee. ______

Definition: ⓐ *adj.* usual ⓑ *n.* normal procedure

2 My uncle is a **regular** at this restaurant. He eats here every Friday. ______

The hockey player is just a **regular** guy. He's not famous at all. ______

It rains in Seattle on a **regular** basis. ______

Definition: ⓐ *n.* someone who often goes to the same place ⓑ *adj.* happening often ⓒ *adj.* ordinary, not special

3 I know a great **vegetarian** restaurant. They are well known for their salads. ______

I can't eat this chicken because I'm a **vegetarian**. ______

Definition: ⓐ *n.* someone who does not eat meat ⓑ *adj.* without meat

B. Word Definitions

Use the clues to fill in the blanks with the word choices given. Change the word form if necessary.

myth	effective	discover	consume	notion	research

1. This is a(n) ____________ treatment for cancer. The doctor says it will work. (useful)
2. Most popular scientific theories began as simple ____________. (concept)
3. Researchers work hard to ____________ cures for various diseases. (uncover)
4. You won't get sick from being outside in cold weather. That is a(n) ____________. (rumor)
5. Dr. Morgan is ____________ the history of Egypt. (study)
6. ____________ too much food is unhealthy. (eat)

C. Multiple Choice

Circle the correct answers.

1. According to the writer, what does eating before bed do?
   a. It makes you fat.
   b. It helps you go to sleep.
   c. It causes you to be healthy.
   d. It does nothing.

2. Which of the following statements is true?
   a. All soda can affect your health.
   b. Only regular soda is bad for you.
   c. Diet soda will make you lose weight.
   d. You shouldn't worry about how much diet soda you drink.

3. Why are diet drinks unhealthy?
   a. They will burn off calories.
   b. They can give you diabetes.
   c. They have too much protein.
   d. They don't allow you to build muscle.

4. If you want to build muscle, it is helpful to eat ____________.
   a. a lot
   b. only meat
   c. protein
   d. salads

UNIT 4

Close Ties

Think of all the important people in your life. Your friends and family help you get through problems. Which relationships are most important to you?

Words & Expressions

Task I *Listen to the two people talking about their relationships. Which one has filled in this form?* Track 14

Speaker 1:
Deborah

Speaker 2:
Alan

Question	True	False	It depends.
1. Arguments can be positive in a relationship.	✓		
2. I'm seeing someone at the moment.	✓		
3. Friendship is more important than family.		✓	
4. You should be frank with everyone.			✓
5. I have a close relationship with my family.	✓		
6. It's important that my family and partner get along.	✓		
7. Colleagues shouldn't become close friends.		✓	

Chat with Your Partner:

1. Which person are you most like? In what way?
2. Do you prefer to keep different parts of your life separate?

Task II *Use the correct form of the words given to complete the sentences.*

relationship	argument	see	friendship
frank	get along	colleague	

1. Pete and Anne fight all the time. Their ______________ is not going to last forever.
2. Gary is ______________ about his feelings. He says what he feels.
3. Pamela is ______________ a new guy. He seems pretty nice.
4. Sometimes, my ______________ gives me a ride to our office in the morning.
5. Teenagers often get into ______________ with their parents.
6. I don't ______________ with Linda's parents. Spending time with them is difficult.
7. Some people don't believe that ______________ between a man and a woman is possible.

Listen Up

*Listen and check **True** or **False**.* Track 15

	True	False
1. The man and his wife are happily married.	☐	☐
2. They were faithful to each other.	☐	☐
3. They argued a lot.	☐	☐
4. They spent time together at work.	☐	☐
5. They spoke less and less.	☐	☐
6. The man apologized for not spending enough time with her.	☐	☐

Language Tip

*The word **date** has many different meanings. Match each usage with its definition.*

_____ 1. What's the **date** of your graduation party?
_____ 2. The two couples went on a double **date**.
_____ 3. Emily's **date** is an attractive guy.
_____ 4. Ken is **dating** someone from work right now.

a. *v.* to have a relationship with
b. *n.* a romantic meeting
c. *n.* a day of the year
d. *n.* a person you are seeing

Class Interview

What do you and your partner think is most important for a good relationship? Do you agree?

	The Secret to a Good Relationship	You	Your Partner
1	You communicate well with each other.		
2	You feel comfortable around each other.		
3	You spend time together.		
4	You are willing to admit a mistake and make an apology.		
5	You should never cheat on each other.		

Ask your other classmates what is most important to them using different words. Fill in the chart.

Statement
1. __________ thinks that hanging out is the most important thing.
2. __________ believes that you should always be faithful.
3. __________ says that talking is the key to a healthy relationship.
4. __________ thinks that you need to be able to relax together.
5. Saying sorry is most important to __________.

Conversation

The Breakup

Fill in the blanks with the word choices given. Then listen to check your answers. Track 16

charming	crying	argument	lies	attracted

Anita goes to Melanie's house and knocks at the door.

Anita: Hello, Melanie. It's Anita!

Melanie: One second!

(Melanie opens the door.)

Anita: You're not **1.** __________, are you?

Melanie: I'm fine. I was just in the kitchen.

Anita: Come on. You can tell me what's going on.

Melanie: I split up with Tony.

Anita: No way. I thought you two were falling in love.

Melanie: Well, not really. We only went out a few times.

Anita: But I thought it was going well. He was **2.** __________.

Melanie: Well, I was **3.** __________ to him, but he was kind of dull. He only ever talked about sports. It was boring hanging out with him. We couldn't communicate.

Anita: He plays hockey, doesn't he?

Melanie: That's right. I always came second to sports. It wasn't working out anyway. He also lied all the time.

Anita: You're kidding! Really?

Melanie: Yeah. They weren't even good **4.** __________. He just said things to make himself sound more interesting. It wasn't very romantic.

Anita: Wow. You really didn't like him, did you?

Melanie: No. Our **5.** __________ just now was about food. He's obviously a terrible chef. I couldn't stand being with a man like that, could I?

Anita: So why are you so upset?

Melanie: I was chopping the onions when I dumped him.

A. Meanings in Context

Choose the meaning of the sentence in the conversation.

1. I split up with Tony. **a.** I am not in a relationship with Tony anymore. **b.** Tony and I break things together.	**2.** We only went out a few times. **a.** We went outside only a few times. **b.** We only went on a few dates.
3. It was boring hanging out with him. **a.** Being with him was not exciting. **b.** We didn't like being out of the house.	**4.** I always came second to sports. **a.** He didn't put me first. **b.** I never placed first in sports.
5. It wasn't working out anyway. **a.** I didn't like exercising. **b.** Our relationship was failing.	**6.** He's obviously a terrible chef. **a.** It's clear that he is bad at cooking. **b.** He is a very bad leader.

B. Word Definitions

Use the clues to fill in the blanks with the word choices given. Change the word form if necessary.

breakup	charming	be attracted to
communicate	upset	dump

1. He's crying upstairs; I think he's ______________. (unhappy)
2. She ______________ Justin because she found him to be very handsome. (feel drawn to)
3. After she cheated on him, he ______________ her. (end the relationship with)
4. We speak different languages, so it's difficult to ______________. (get across information)
5. He was trying hard to get back together with her after the ______________. (end of the relationship)
6. You will like her once you talk to her. She is a ______________ girl. (attractive)

C. Expressions

Expressing Surprise

weaker →		stronger
Really? Wow. No way. For real / sure?	You're kidding! Get out of here!	That's amazing! I can't believe it! That's incredible!

Respond to the following with the expressions above. Use different expressions for each one.

1. **A:** Check out my new scooter. I bought it yesterday. **B:** ______________
2. **A:** I just got promoted to the position of sales manager. **B:** ______________
3. **A:** The store is selling TVs at 60 percent off. **B:** ______________
4. **A:** Dr. Watts does over 400 surgeries a year. **B:** ______________

Grammar

Tag Questions

Tag questions are statements followed by small questions. They usually have the same use as "Right?" We want to confirm what we said with the other person.

Basic Structure

Positive Statement (+)	Negative Tag (-)
He plays hockey, They have a problem, The refrigerator is broken, You'll be there, We're going to start at 5:00 p.m., Annie came home late yesterday,	doesn't he? don't they? isn't it? won't you? aren't we? didn't she?
Negative Statement (-)	**Positive Tag (+)**
You're not crying, You really didn't like him, I couldn't stand being with a man like that, She shouldn't be here, There isn't any food left, It can't be true,	are you? did you? could I? should she? is there? can it?

Usage Note

The auxiliary verb should match the statement. Think about the full question you would make. Answer tag questions just like normal questions.

For Example:

A: You like cake, don't you? (Don't you like cake?)

B: Yes, I do. Cheesecake is my favorite. / No, I don't. I try to avoid desserts.

Special Cases

Rule	Example
For **nobody, someone,** or **everybody,** use **they**.	Nobody knows, do they? Everybody agrees, don't they?
For **something** or **nothing**, use **it**.	Something happened, didn't it? Nothing came in today, did it?
For **used to**, use **didn't**.	You used to play football, didn't you?
For requests, use **will / would you**.	Close the door, will you? Pass me the salt, would you? (more polite)

A. Fill in the Blanks

Write the correct tag to complete the sentences.

1. Your wife wasn't too happy about the situation, ______________?
2. They are going to go to Spain this summer, ______________?
3. We don't have any tea in the house, ______________?
4. Nobody saw him come into the office today, ______________?
5. Help me carry this box into the other room, ______________?
6. Matt used to be a boxing champion, ______________?

B. Match

Match the tag question with the most appropriate response.

____ 1. You're on TV, aren't you?
____ 2. We've met before, haven't we?
____ 3. They're coming tonight, aren't they?
____ 4. She's going to college, isn't she?
____ 5. You'll be at home tonight, won't you?
____ 6. I don't have any water, do I?
____ 7. We didn't start early enough, did we?
____ 8. I won't have time, will I?

a. Yes, we have. At Sharon's birthday party.
b. No. We'll never get it finished on time.
c. Yes, I will. From six p.m. on.
d. No. You left the bottle at the campsite.
e. Yes, I am. I report the news.
f. Yes, you will. Just leave now.
g. No, they're not. They're out of town.
h. Yes. I think she's studying medicine.

C. Complete the Dialogues

Write the correct tag and response to complete each dialogue.

1. Q You haven't finished that book yet, __________?
   A ________________. It's very long.

2. Q There's a park nearby, __________?
   A ________________. It should be around this corner.

3. Q I'm talking too much, __________?
   A ________________. You're usually very quiet.

4. Q We should take a taxi, __________?
   A ________________. Or, we'll miss our flight.

5. Q There isn't much pork left, __________?
   A ________________. I used most of it yesterday.

6. Q You won't be gone long, __________?
   A ________________. The store is close by.

7. Q They prefer Chinese food, __________?
   A ________________. Let's make fried rice for them.

8. Q You don't know where the library is, __________?
   A ________________. Just take the next left.

Reading

Before You Read *Discuss the following questions with a partner:*

1. What are some dating customs in your country?
2. Do you know any dating traditions in other countries?

Dating around the World

Track 17

Dating a foreigner can be a wonderful experience, but it might also present challenges. Take a look at these dating customs from various countries:

Kim, age 20, Korea

"In Korea, students are busy and tend to wait until college to begin dating. It is customary for the man to pay on a date. If a guy asks a girl to 'go Dutch', she won't think he's interested in her. However, if they get coffee after the date, the girl will usually offer to pay for it."

Jack, age 22, India

"In the past, most marriages in India were arranged by the parents of the spouses. Sometimes, the bride and groom didn't meet until their wedding day. However, this custom is slightly less common in India today. My parents let me decide who I want to date."

Pedro, age 18, Nicaragua

"Central America is rather conservative. Teens usually aren't allowed to date until they're 15 years old. In my country, people don't date in pairs. Instead, a large group might go to a dance party together. This makes dating a bit more relaxed."

Karen, age 20, Germany

"In Germany, it's important to be on time for a date. If you're late, the date might get cancelled. We do have one interesting custom. When a guy picks a girl up at her house, he should bring flowers for the girl ... and her mother!"

A. Words with Different Meanings

Match the word in bold with its definition.

1 Jane is still missing at the **present** moment, but we will continue looking for her. ______

Large class sizes sometimes **present** problems for students. ______

Definition: ⓐ *v.* to give ⓑ *adj.* current

2 That steep mountain is a **challenge** for any climber. ______

I told Carl that I was good at tennis, so he **challenged** me to a game. ______

Definition: ⓐ *n.* something difficult ⓑ *v.* to invite to compete

3 If you try to bring drugs into the country, **Customs** will stop you. ______

In her culture, it's a **custom** to exchange gifts when you first meet. ______

Definition: ⓐ *n.* a tradition ⓑ *n.* the agency that monitors goods coming into a country

B. Word Definitions

Use the clues to fill in the blanks with the word choices given. Change the word form if necessary.

various	customary	go Dutch	tend to
marriage	arrange	conservative	allow

1. Her parents are ______________. They don't allow her to go out past ten p.m. (traditional)
2. At Amy's university, boys are not ______________ in the girls' dormitory. (permit)
3. My grandparents' ______________ lasted until they died. (the union of husband and wife)
4. Why don't we ______________ on the bill? We can each pay half. (split the cost)
5. The lawyer ______________ a meeting with his client yesterday. (coordinate)
6. We have ______________ kinds of cereal in aisle six. (different)
7. The man is old, and he ______________ forget certain things. (is likely to)
8. In America, it is ______________ to shake someone's hand when you first meet them. (typical)

C. Multiple Choice

Circle the correct answers.

1. When do Korean students start dating?
   a. in high school
   b. in primary school
   c. during college
   d. when they are middle aged

2. In the past, who arranged most marriages in India?
   a. an uncle on the bride's side
   b. the groom's father
   c. the government
   d. fathers and mothers

3. How do people date in Nicaragua?
   a. People find dates online.
   b. Large groups go to events together.
   c. Companies arrange date nights.
   d. People date only in pairs.

4. To whom must a German boy bring flowers when he goes on a date?
   a. the girl and her mother
   b. all of the girls in the family
   c. the girl and her entire family
   d. the girl's father

UNIT 5

Time to Celebrate

Sometimes life becomes so busy that you don't st enjoy it. Let's take some time to explore how peo over the world have fun.

Words & Expressions

Task I *Listen and use the words given to fill in the blanks in the postcard.* Track 18

exciting	fight	Thousands	covered	last week

August 28th

Hey Sarah,

Spain has been terrific! I was in Madrid ❶ __________, and now I'm in the town of Buñol. It's home to the most well-known food ❷ __________ in the world. ❸ __________ of people came to take part in *La Tomatina*. The night before the festival, the shop owners all ❹ __________ their shops to prepare for the holiday. We all drank wine and ate great food to get ready to participate in the battle. The next morning, the town's narrow streets were filled with people. More than 150,000 tomatoes were thrown around. Unlike some other celebrations, no one wore costumes. They just put on clothes that they didn't care about. It was the most ❺ __________ moment in my whole life!

Jess

Photo: flydime / Flickr

Task II *Find the matching words from the postcard for the following.*

1. party: __________	2. special clothes: __________	3. fantastic: __________	4. participate in: __________
5. famous: __________	6. be full of: __________	7. fight: __________	8. joyful event: __________

Task III *Use the words from **Task II** to fill in the blanks.*

1. Sharon wore a witch __________ for Halloween.
2. She's going to __________ the dance show next week.
3. The soldiers were preparing their weapons for the __________.
4. I hope you're coming to Emily's birthday party. We're planning a big __________.
5. He is a(n) __________ scientist. He often appears on TV programs about science.
6. Our town's __________ is a whole week of fun and games.

Listen Up

Listen and complete the chart. Track 19

Festival	*Holi*	*Hadaka Matsuri*
Where is the festival from?	____________	____________
What can we say about the festival?	☐ active ☐ violent	☐ too dark to see ☐ amazing to see
What do the people do?	They throw ________.	They get ________.

Language Tip

There are different ways to say a place is crowded:

(a place)	be filled with be full of be packed with	(a lot of people)

Fill in the blanks with the phrases above. Practice saying the sentences with a partner.

1. The party was a great success! The house ____________ people.
2. The zoo is usually ____________ visitors at this time.

Class Interview

Ask one of your classmates the following questions.

Question
1. What do you think is the most extraordinary festival?
2. Do you prefer religious festivals or nonreligious festivals?
3. If you could choose between a feast and a parade, which one would you pick?
4. Is the Lunar New Year an energetic festival?
5. How many annual festivals can you name?

Match the expressions above with those below. Write the student's name and share with the class.

Statement
1. ____________ prefers having a large meal to walking through the streets.
2. ____________ likes festivals which are connected to gods.
3. If you want to know about festivals that happen every year, ask ____________.
4. ____________ thinks that ____________ is the most amazing festival.
5. The Lunar New Year isn't a very active time for ____________.

Conversation

The Road to Mexico

Fill in the blanks with the word choices given. Then listen to check your answers. Track 20

festival	travel agency	costumes	booked	time

Pedro and Debbie are outside the university.

Debbie: Hi, Pedro! How are you?

Pedro: Good! I just **1.** __________ a flight home.

Debbie: Oh, that slipped my mind. You're going back for Carnival, right?

Pedro: Yes. It's a **2.** __________ that we have every year.

Debbie: That sounds fun. Do you have to be religious to participate?

Pedro: No. Anybody can join in. Would you like to come? There's still **3.** __________.

Debbie: That would be great. What do you usually do?

Pedro: We normally have a parade, wear **4.** __________, and dance. There's music too. We'll have a great time!

Debbie: Oh, you remember Jenny, right? She said she was going to Carnival too!

Pedro: Um ... I forget.

Debbie: You know. She's the girl whom we bumped into last Tuesday. We met her in the library.

Pedro: Oh yeah. How about we all go together? I can show you the traditional stuff in the community.

Debbie: Count me in. We'll have a ball! Where did you buy your tickets?

Pedro: I got them from a **5.** __________ that I found on the Internet. I'll show you the site.

A. Word Definitions

Use the clues to fill in the blanks with the word choices given.

carnival	normally	parade	traditional	community	travel agency

1. I love my ______________. People there always help each other out. (neighborhood)
2. The ______________ begins at City Hall and finishes at the library. (walk)
3. Turkey is a ______________ dish people serve on Thanksgiving. (typical)
4. Each year, people dress up and party in the streets. It's called a ______________. (outdoor celebration)
5. Someone from the ______________ called today. You still haven't paid for the plane tickets. (holiday company)
6. I live close to the university. It ______________ takes me 15 minutes to get to school. (usually)

B. Meanings in Context

Choose the meaning of the sentence in the conversation.

1. Oh, that slipped my mind.
   a. Nobody told me.
   b. I completely forgot.

2. Do you have to be religious to participate?
   a. Do you have to believe in God to join in?
   b. Do you need to take part in a church?

3. She's the girl whom we bumped into last Tuesday.
   a. We hit that girl last week.
   b. We met the girl last week.

4. I can show you the traditional stuff in the community.
   a. I can take you to see the typical neighborhood activities.
   b. I can show you the history of the country.

5. Count me in.
   a. I need help. I'm not good at math.
   b. Great! I would love to come.

6. We'll have a ball!
   a. We will play sports.
   b. It's going to be fun.

C. Expressions

Making and Responding to Invitations

Making an Invitation	Accepting an Invitation	Declining an Invitation
Would you like to + Verb?	That would be great.	Can I take a rain check?
How / What about + Subject + Verb?	Count me in.	I'll have to pass.
How / What about + Verb + -ing?	I'm in.	No, thanks. I'm busy that day.
Do you want to + Verb?	I'd love to. Thanks.	I'm sorry. I already have plans.
Do you feel like + Verb + -ing?	Sounds good.	

Make short dialogues using the word choices below. Student A is inviting student B to do something.

Student A	see a show	go for a jog	grab a bite to eat	go bowling
Student B	accept	decline	accept	decline

A: I'm going to see a show with some friends later. **Would you like to** join us?
B: I'm sorry. I already have plans.

Grammar

Relative Clauses

Put relative clauses after nouns to give more information. The relative clause contains a subject and a verb, and it begins with a relative pronoun.

Relative Pronouns

	Use	Example
who	subject pronoun for people	Do you know the people who live next door?
which	subject or object pronoun for things	There's a path which leads to the woods.
whose	possession for people and things	Are you the person whose bag was stolen?
that	subject or object pronoun for people and things	It's a festival that we have every year.

Usage Note

1. **Whom** is the object pronoun for people. It is often used in written English.
   Dan is the guy **whom** I had dinner with yesterday.
2. **That** is usually used after superlatives and words like **all**, **much**, and **only**.
   It's the best book **that** I have ever read.

Relative Pronoun Reduction

Relative pronouns can only be removed when they are the **object** of the clause.

Example	Is the relative pronoun required?
She's the girl (whom / that) we bumped into.	no; it's the object of *bumped into*
Oil is a product which / that has changed the world.	yes; it's the subject of *has changed*

Prepositions in Relative Clauses

When a prepositional phrase is involved, there are three different ways of combining two sentences with a relative clause.

I went to a store. + I bought a tie from the store.

Preposition at the end	I went to a store that / which I bought a tie from.
Preposition and object to the front (Here, you have to use **which**.)	I went to a store from which I bought a tie.
Remove the object pronoun. (The preposition must be kept at the end.)	I went to a store I bought a tie from.

A. Fill in the Blanks

Fill in the correct relative pronoun. For some questions, more than one answer is correct.

1. Did you see the man ________________ was here a minute ago?
2. There are two roads ________________ we can take.
3. I don't know the woman ________________ car is parked outside.
4. Mandy is meeting someone ________________ she knew in college.
5. I haven't read the article ________________ he's talking about.
6. There is much information ________________ we do not have.
7. He lives in the apartment ________________ is on the top floor.
8. The house in ________________ Sally lives is near the park.

B. Combine the Sentences

Connect the two sentences using a relative clause.

1. I met a pretty girl yesterday. The pretty girl was Joe's sister.
   → The pretty girl ____.
2. I like the kids. They live on my street.
   → I like ____.
3. Near my place, there's a building. It has no windows.
   → Near my place, ____.
4. Kevin has a new friend. His friend's dad is a police officer.
   → Kevin has ____.
5. The boy wants to go home. He is called Ray.
   → The boy ____.
6. We went to the town. The festival was held in the town.
   → We went ____.

C. Correct the Mistakes

Fix the errors in the passage.

which / that / X

The place ~~who~~ I come from is small and quiet. In the village, there are people whose their houses have been in the family for hundreds of years. Most of the people are friendly, and they always know everything whose happens in the area. I do the shopping for the woman whom lives next door. She is kind and often bakes us bread has nuts and fruit. I like the feeling of community, so I help anyone who house needs cleaning. I really prefer to live in the countryside. I lived in the city for a long time. I'm glad to be back!

Reading

Before You Read *Discuss the following questions with a partner:*

1. What are some of your favorite holiday traditions?
2. How might some of your culture's traditions seem strange to an outsider?

America's Unique Festivals

Track 21

America is made up of people from many different cultures, so it has a variety of festivals and celebrations. Holidays such as Thanksgiving and the Fourth of July are known almost everywhere, but some festivals in America are not as well known. These festivals are often considered both fun and strange.

Many festivals are born out of a town's unique history. For example, a festival in Wisconsin helps people to recall the time that pioneers moved west in the 19th century. The pioneers used cow droppings as fuel for their fires and called them "cow chips." Today, the Wisconsin State Cow Chip Throw & Festival holds a contest to see who can throw a cow chip the farthest.

Some people might consider Groundhog Day to be one of the strangest American celebrations. This holiday is celebrated all over the country. Long ago, people waited for the warm spring weather after a long winter. According to tradition, groundhogs could predict how long the winter would last. Today, the most famous groundhog is named Punxsutawney Phil. Every February second, Phil "whispers" his prediction to the Groundhog Club president, and the president announces it to the crowd. Phil's fans say he's never wrong.

However, not every festival in America has historical roots. Some festivals have unusual contests just for fun. One instance occurs in Oatman, Arizona, where it can get up to 40 degrees Celsius. At the Oatman Sidewalk Egg Frying Contest, people compete to see who can fry the most edible-looking egg on the sidewalk.

America is filled with many odd festivals. These events make the nation unique and celebrate its diverse culture.

A. Fill in the Blanks

Use the word choices given to complete the sentences. Change the word form if necessary.

strange	unique	contest	root	announce	diverse

1. I always get excited before they ____________ the winners at the Oscar Awards.
2. Our family has ____________ in Ireland. My grandfather came here 80 years ago.
3. His garden is very ____________. It has many different herbs and vegetables.
4. Your father doesn't like your blue hair. He thinks it's ____________.
5. This painting is so ____________. It's truly one of a kind.
6. The ____________ begins at eight a.m. The first team to get 100 points will win.

B. Words with Different Meanings

Match the word in bold with its definition.

1 Do you know who **pioneered** the Internet? ______

Albert Einstein was a **pioneer** of early modern science. ______

Definition: ⓐ *n.* a person that invents something or leads the way

ⓑ *v.* to invent something or do it first

2 My dad had to stop the car because it ran out of **fuel**. ______

These workers are not happy with their pay. This is **fueling** their anger. ______

Definition: ⓐ *n.* something that provides energy ⓑ *v.* to make something grow larger

3 Stop **whispering**. I can't hear you. ______

Diane spoke in a **whisper** because she didn't want us to hear her secret. ______

Definition: ⓐ *n.* a quiet voice ⓑ *v.* to say something quietly

C. Multiple Choice

Circle the correct answers.

1. Why does America have many festivals?
   a. Americans love to have fun.
   b. It consists of many different kinds of people.
   c. It has the funniest people in the world.
   d. The towns of America are unique.

2. What made the fires of pioneers special?
   a. the fuel
   b. the size
   c. the color
   d. the history

3. Why do the people of Oatman, Arizona, hold a festival?
   a. They want to celebrate their history.
   b. They really like eating fried eggs.
   c. They are joking about the hot weather.
   d. They have very clean sidewalks.

4. What do groundhogs predict?
   a. the start of winter
   b. the length of winter
   c. the snowfall
   d. the middle of summer

UNIT 6

A Fine Art

Art used to be only for the rich. In modern times available to everyone. The Internet and museums opened the doors of the art world to all. Jump in!

Words & Expressions

Task I *Listen and choose the correct words used from the options below.* Track 22

The Joseph Stark Art ❶ ____________ [Museum, Show, Gallery] is holding a new exhibition.

Frida Kahlo — Her Life and Art

You will see more than 30 of her ❷ ____________ [portraits, masterpieces, paintings] on ❸ ____________ [show, exhibit, display]. Frida Kahlo (1907 – 1954) is a highly ❹ ____________ [influential / powerful / artistic] painter of the 20th century. Her ❺ ____________ [problem, health, life] was bad. That's why many of her paintings ❻ ____________ [paint, express, impress] pain. People in Mexico see her as a ❼ ____________ [normal, famous, national] hero. Many modern artists admire her works, especially her portraits.

On opening night, art scholar Alberto Garcia will talk about her life story.
Opens on December 1st.

Free ❽ ____________ [addition, admission, admiration]!

Task II *Use the words given to complete the sentences.*

express	scholar	exhibition	masterpiece	on display
admission	gallery	influential	admire	portrait

1. Many modern scientists use Newton's ideas. Even today, he is very ____________.
2. The photographs will be ____________ for the whole weekend.
3. The price of ____________ to the movie is $9.
4. He doesn't know how to ____________ his feelings in words.
5. The *Mona Lisa* was da Vinci's ____________.
6. Professor Connelly has studied history all his life. He is an important ____________.
7. I want to check out this ____________ of Japanese art at the museum.
8. The artist painted a(n) ____________ of the old woman.
9. There is a new collection of paintings at the ____________.
10. I really ____________ Mary. She works so hard.

Listen Up

*Listen and check **True** or **False**.* Track 23

	True	False
1. Wassily Kandinsky was an important painter from Russia.	☐	☐
2. Kandinsky's paintings are realistic.	☐	☐
3. Kandinsky painted with oil on canvas.	☐	☐
4. Most of Antoni Gaudí's buildings are in Barcelona.	☐	☐
5. Gaudí used colors in traditional ways.	☐	☐
6. Gaudí's designs expressed his love for nature.	☐	☐

Casa Milà, Antoni Gaudí

Language Tip

*Do you know the difference between **work**, **work of art**, and **masterpiece**? Fill in the chart.*

	the general work of an artist or any piece of art
	an artist's best piece of art
	any piece of art

Complete the sentences with the appropriate words. More than one answer is possible.

1. I like all of his work, but I think this is his ____________.
2. Let's go to the museum and see some ____________.
3. This painting is a beautiful ____________.

Class Interview

*Find a classmate who answers **yes** to the questions below.*

Do you like ...	Classmate
1. pretty vases?	____________
2. paintings that are not similar to real life?	____________
3. realistic, traditional stonework?	____________
4. beautiful buildings?	____________
5. interesting photos?	____________

Study for Composition VII, Wassily Kandinsky

Match the expressions above with those below. List the classmate's name in the appropriate blank.

Statement	
1. ____________ likes pottery art.	2. ____________ prefers architecture.
3. ____________ appreciates photography.	4. ____________ loves abstract paintings.
5. ____________ admires sculpture.	

Conversation

Looking at Art

Fill in the blanks with the word choices given. Then listen to check your answers. Track 24

prohibited	impress	exhibit	talent	definitely	masterpiece

Chad and Lisa are walking through an art museum.

Chad: This is a great display.

Lisa: Yeah. If I had as much **1.** __________ as this artist, I would be rich.

Chad: Well, I think you have a gift for art. Look at this painting. It's a(n) **2.** __________.

Lisa: I don't care for this one. It doesn't **3.** __________ me.

Chad: I admire the artist's ability to paint landscapes. She has a natural talent for it.

Lisa: If I had the money, I would collect art. That's a perfect life for me.

Chad: Do you think I can take a picture of this painting? Will the guards be annoyed?

Lisa: The use of cameras is **4.** __________. If you take a picture, they'll be angry!

Chad: Alright. Sorry. I'm glad you appreciate art. If you didn't join me, I wouldn't come to an exhibition like this.

Lisa: We should go to another **5.** __________ next week. I hear that it's one of a kind.

Chad: Whose work will be on display?

Lisa: An abstract artist's. My roommate says that he's fantastic.

Chad: Well, in my opinion, abstract art is nothing special. But if I have free time, I'll **6.** __________ go.

Lisa: Great! Also, students are allowed to bring a friend for free.

Chad: Let's do it!

A. Word Definitions

Use the clues to fill in the blanks with the word choices given. Change the word form if necessary.

gift | care for | impress | landscape | annoy | prohibit | in one's opinion

1. Gina doesn't ______________ cold weather. (like)
2. Jimmy has a(n) ______________ for music. He learned how to play the guitar very quickly. (natural ability)
3. That mosquito is really ______________ me! I can't stand it! (bother)
4. The ______________ in the country is beautiful. Look at the trees and mountains. (natural scenery)
5. Eddie ______________ his teacher with a high score on his test. (make one think highly of you)
6. Most movie theaters ______________ smoking. (not allow)
7. ______________, the only good thing about *Avatar* is the special effects. (I think)

B. Words with Different Meanings

Match the word in bold with its definition.

1
They held a fantastic firework **display** to celebrate the New Year. ______
The sculptor **displayed** his work in the new exhibition hall downtown. ______
Definition: ⓐ *v.* to show ⓑ *n.* a group of things in a show

2
Someone broke into the building, so the security **guard** called the police. ______
We wanted to go in, but two men were **guarding** the door. ______
Definition: ⓐ *n.* a person who protects something ⓑ *v.* to protect

3
We **appreciate** that you're having problems. ______
I **appreciate** your honesty. It's useful to have your thoughts on the matter. ______
Joe really **appreciates** fine wines. ______
Definition: ⓐ *v.* to recognize value ⓑ *v.* to realize ⓒ *v.* to feel thankful for

C. Expressions

Talking about Natural Talents

have a gift for	show a talent for
have a natural talent for	be a talented / gifted / natural + Noun
be naturally good at	

Use the words below to practice the expressions above. Change the word form if necessary.

leadership | sculpture | public | speaking | sales | songwriter | actor

Eric **has a natural talent for** leadership.
Eric **is naturally good at** leading people.
Eric **is a gifted** leader.

Grammar

Factual and Unreal Conditionals

Summary

	Zero Conditional	First Conditional	Second Conditional
Usage	present facts (certain)	possible future results (likely)	unreal events (unlikely or impossible)
Form	If (When / Every time) + simple present, simple present.	If + simple present, will / can / may / should / might / must + Verb.	If + simple past, would / could / might + Verb.
Example	If Sally eats seafood, she gets sick. If Phil visits his grandma, he brings a book to read to her.	If you take a picture, they'll be angry. If I have free time, I'll definitely go.	If I had as much talent as this artist, I would be rich. If I had the money, I would collect art. If you didn't join me, I wouldn't come to an exhibition like this.

Compare the two examples below:

Example	Explanation
If I have enough money, I will go to Europe.	It's likely that I will have enough money. In that case, I will go to Europe.
If I had enough money, I would go to Europe.	I'd like to go to Europe, but it's unlikely that I'll have enough money.

Different Forms

First Conditional

Usage	Form	Example
Action going on now	If + simple present continuous, will + Verb.	If Mary is talking loudly, I will tell her to speak more quietly.
Finished action	If + simple present perfect, will + Verb.	If Greg has finished packing, we will leave.

A. Match

Match the two parts.

1.	If I had his e-mail,	if he knew how.
2.	Mr. Lee would fix it	they last longer.
3.	I wouldn't ask for his opinion	I'll call back later.
4.	If we had a bigger house,	you will lose weight.
5.	You would make more money	if he just studied a little more.
6.	If you're eating dinner,	if she didn't buy so many shoes.
7.	If you exercise more,	I would write to him.
8.	My son could get good grades	if I were you.
9.	Cindy would save money	we could keep a dog.
10.	If you buy better clothes,	if you worked harder.

B. Fill in the Blanks

Use the correct form of the verbs in parentheses to complete the sentences.

1. If he ______________ (have) a million dollars, he ______________ (buy) a new car.
2. If I ______________ (pass) the test, I ______________ (be) very happy.
3. She ______________ (have) to buy another ticket if she ______________ (miss) the plane.
4. If time ______________ (permit), I ______________ (stop) by your house next week.
5. If you ______________ (go) to the party tomorrow, you ______________ (enjoy) yourself.
6. If it ______________ (rain), I ______________ (cancel) the picnic.
7. If you ______________ (lose) your job, how ______________ you ______________ (pay) the rent?
8. I can't ______________ (take) a vacation if I ______________ (not have) any time off.

C. Correct the Mistakes

Fix the errors in the passage.

A lot of people dream about winning the lottery. They say that if they ~~wins~~ won the lottery, their lives be perfect. If you winning the lottery, what would you do? Most people would want to quit their jobs. Others say that they to travel the world. However, if you had lots of money, will you be happy? Most people say *yes*, but some disagree. If you have lots of money, you might not be happy. After all, if you having all that free time, how would you stay busy? Will you be bored? That's the danger of having too much money. If you are bored, you wouldn't be happy. So the next time you wish that you were rich, think twice!

Reading

Before You Read *Discuss the following questions with a partner:*

1. How often do you visit museums?
2. What kind of art do you enjoy? Which special museums would you like to visit?

The World's Most Uncommon Museums

Track 25

Museums are often a part of tourists' travel itinerary. Most sightseers flock to see historic paintings, fine art, and elaborate sculptures, but have you ever considered visiting some unconventional museums? If you took a trip across the globe, you could find museums featuring nearly any object that you could dream of!

Let's begin in Asia. Most people wouldn't consider ramen noodles to be very note-worthy, but Japan holds an entire museum dedicated to the history and production of this popular food. Thc museum highlights bowls, chopsticks, and instruments necessary to manufacture ramen noodles. It even has an entire floor that resembles Tokyo in 1958, the year that ramen was first sold in stores.

If you explored Europe next, you could find several notable torture museums. The Netherlands, Belgium, Germany, and Italy all feature a type of torture museum. These museums highlight the torture tools that were common during the Medieval Period when torture was a societal norm.

If you traveled farther east to North America, you would find that the United States has its fair share of odd museums. For example, in Massachusetts, you can find the Museum of Bad Art, which preserves and displays the worst art imaginable. Another interesting museum, called Miniature World, is found in British Columbia, Canada. This museum features doll houses, model railways, and small replicas of British castles.

The next time you map out your vacation, why not broaden your perspective and explore some interesting museums? You could satisfy your curiosity and have fun!

A. Words with Different Meanings

Match the word in bold with its definition.

1 This **object** is too heavy for me to lift. ______

The **object** of this meeting is to solve our problem. ______

Why did you **object** to our idea? ______

Definition: **a** *n.* a thing **b** *v.* to oppose or disagree **c** *n.* the purpose of something

2 You can't **preserve** those eggs for very long. ______

The paintings are **preserved** in the museum. ______

Definition: **a** *v.* to keep safe from damage **b** *v.* to store food and keep it fresh

3 A good student will **map** out the course of their studies. ______

The captain relied on his **map** during the journey. ______

Definition: **a** *v.* to plan or plot out **b** *n.* a geographical diagram

B. Word Definitions

Use the clues to fill in the blanks with the word choices given. Change the word form if necessary.

tourist	itinerary	instrument	notable	imaginable	broaden

1. This ____________ is used to make bread. (tool)
2. Every year, many ____________ travel to France. (someone on vacation)
3. When Jim traveled to Poland for business, he had a very full ____________. (travel plan)
4. That is the best plan ____________! I'll never come up with something better. (thinkable)
5. Construction workers plan to ____________ the road that leads into the city. (widen)
6. The *Mona Lisa* is a ____________ work of art. (significant)

C. Multiple Choice

Circle the correct answers.

1. What does the Ramen Museum display?
- **a.** traditional Japanese art
- **b.** traditional Japanese buildings
- **c.** traditional Japanese clothing
- **d.** a type of traditional Japanese food

2. Which museum would most likely feature ugly paintings?
- **a.** the Ramen Museum
- **b.** the Museum of Torture
- **c.** the Museum of Bad Art
- **d.** Miniature World

3. Where is the Museum of Bad Art located?
- **a.** on America's east coast
- **b.** in central Europe
- **c.** close to Tokyo, Japan
- **d.** in the middle of Canada

4. Which of the following statements is false?
- **a.** The Ramen Museum displays instruments used to make ramen.
- **b.** There is more than one torture museum in Europe.
- **c.** Miniature World is located in North America.
- **d.** The author suggests visiting museums that have historic paintings.

UNIT 7

Tune In

American journalist Edward R. Murrow once said television could be either a valuable teaching to simply entertainment. Which do you think it is tod

Words & Expressions

Task I *Look at the TV schedule. Listen and answer the questions below.* Track 26

	Monday	Tuesday	Wednesday	Thursday	Friday
18:00	News	News	News	News	News
19:00	Home Town	Animal Central	Home Town	The View	Home Town
20:00	In the Game	Human Planet	Quiz Show	Live Sports	Movie: Trip to the Stars
21:00	Movie: Dr. Hall	The Report	Stand-up Comedy		
22:00		Real Lives		Real Lives	Real Lives
23:00	Real Lives		Sitcom		

1. Who's TV schedule is this?
   a. Daisy
   b. Chris

2. Why doesn't Daisy like late-night television?
   a. It's mostly educational.
   b. It's about outer space.
   c. She doesn't like comedies.
   d. She says it's silly.

3. What does Chris like about the soap opera?
   a. He loves the narrator.
   b. The characters are interesting.
   c. It's on three times a week.
   d. It teaches him how to cook.

4. Chris does NOT like ______________.
   a. reality series and news
   b. educational shows and news
   c. sports shows and soap operas
   d. soap operas and educational programs

Task II *Use the correct form of the words given to complete the sentences.*

current affairs	educational	comedy	reality
narrator	soap opera	character	viewer

1. This nature show has a great ______________. I like the way she explains what's happening.
2. There's a new ______________ on Channel 45. I couldn't stop laughing.
3. I don't really like the program anymore. All the ______________ have changed.
4. Most ______________ have really dramatic stories. They're difficult to believe.
5. If you want to know about important recent events, you should watch a(n) ______________ show.
6. Many people think that computer games aren't ______________ enough.
7. The baseball game on TV got over 100,000 ______________.
8. ______________ shows are my favorite. You can see how people actually live.

Listen Up

Listen and fill in the blanks. For some questions, more than one answer is correct. Track 27

1. __________ television is amazing because you never know what will __________ next.
2. The speaker __________ many different interesting people on his __________.
3. There used to be fewer __________ 20 years ago.
4. Viewers see lots of cartoons, reality shows, and __________ when they __________.
5. TV programs aren't just for __________; they should give __________ too.

Language Tip

A **series** is a set of TV programs with the same characters. It is on once a week or more. A **season** is shown during a particular time period. These words also have other meanings:

series	a group of events	season	part of the year
	several books with the same topic		usual time for a particular activity

Fill in the blanks with the appropriate words.

1. *The Sopranos* is a __________. It ran for six __________.
2. The __________ for strawberries usually begins in May or June.
3. He has written a __________ of science-fiction novels.
4. The movie *Sex and the City* is based on the popular TV __________ of the same name.

Class Interview

Ask your classmates the following questions.

Do you ...	How do you feel about ...	Would you like to be ...
1. watch any American series?	1. commercials?	1. a talk show host?
2. prefer talk shows or dramas?	2. sitcoms?	2. a couch potato?
3. channel surf?	3. live television?	3. a TV newscaster?

Match the expressions above with those below. Write the student's name and share with the class.

Statement
1. For __________, reading the news is the most interesting job on TV.
2. __________ really doesn't like advertisements.
3. Long-running programs from the U.S. are __________'s favorite.
4. __________ can't stop changing the channel!
5. __________ spends a lot of time watching television.

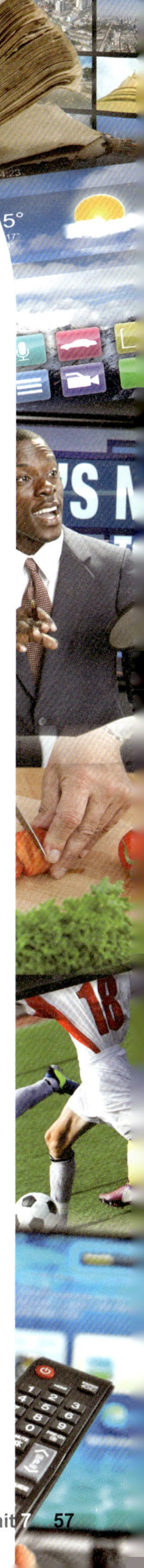

Conversation

What to Watch?

Fill in the blanks with the word choices given. Then listen to check your answers. Track 28

awful	relax	sitcoms	snacks	browsing

Jenny walks into the living room. Paul is watching TV.

Paul: What's up, Jenny? Have you been sleeping this whole time?

Jenny: No. I've been studying all day. I need to **1.** __________.

Paul: I'm going to chill out here for the evening. Do you want to watch television?

Jenny: That would be great. Is there anything good on?

Paul: I've been **2.** __________ the *TV Guide*, but there aren't many options.

Jenny: Well, I'm going to turn it off while you decide. I'm tired of watching commercials.

Paul: No problem. I've been watching them for an hour. The only things on right now are a current affairs show and a talk show.

Jenny: Hmm. They sound too heavy for me. Are there any **3.** __________?

Paul: Well, we could just channel surf and see what we find.

Jenny: I can't stand channel surfing. Give me the *TV Guide*. I'll pick something.

Paul: Yes, boss! You're in the driver's seat.

Jenny: Thanks. Let's see. Oh look! There's a show about famous people on an island.

Paul: Are you talking about that reality show? It's **4.** __________!

Jenny: In that case, we could watch this comedy. It's on in an hour. Will we get **5.** __________?

Paul: You're calling the shots! I'm in.

A. Meanings in Context

Choose the meaning of the sentence in the conversation.

1. I'm going to chill out here for the evening. **a.** If I don't put on a jacket, I'm going to feel cold. **b.** I plan to take it easy and do nothing.	**2.** Is there anything good on? **a.** Is there delicious food on the table? **b.** Are there any interesting TV programs?
3. I'm tired of watching commercials. **a.** Commercials don't interest me now. **b.** Watching commercials makes me sleepy.	**4.** They sound too heavy for me. **a.** They have too many calories. **b.** They are too serious.
5. You're in the driver's seat. **a.** You are the person in control right now. **b.** Be careful not to hit anyone when you drive.	

B. Word Definitions

Use the clues to fill in the blanks with the word choices given. Change the word form if necessary.

browse	option	affairs	reality
awful	in that case	call the shots	

1. Some of you don't want to be in the army. ____________, you can serve your country in another way. (Then)
2. I didn't read the whole story. I just ____________ it for a few minutes. (read quickly)
3. This is a(n) ____________ show about five singers who live together in an apartment. (like life)
4. Reading about the ____________ of the government sometimes makes me angry. (activities)
5. The manager doesn't ____________. Nobody listens to him. (have power)
6. This sandwich tastes ____________. I don't think it's fresh. (very bad)
7. When Beth graduated, she had two ____________. She could start work or go to graduate school. (choice)

C. Expressions

Relaxing

relax	chill out	kick back	loosen up
take it easy	let your hair down	put your feet up	

Create short dialogues using the expressions above and the ideas below.

don't have enough money	haven't had a holiday in a long time
can't finish your essay	have a big race tomorrow

A: I'm really stressed-out! I don't have enough money for the trip to Boston.

B: You need to **chill out**. Maybe your parents could help.

Grammar

Present Perfect Continuous

Form

Statements

Subject	Have / Has	(Not)	Been	Present Participle
I / You / We / They He / She / It	have has	(not) (not)	been been	taking a nap. eating.

Questions

Question
Have you been sleeping this whole time?
Has he been working hard?
What have you been doing?
How long have you been watching commercials?
Why has she been missing school so much?

Response
No. I've been studying all day.
Yes. He's been helping me a lot.
I've been browsing the *TV Guide*.
I've been watching them for an hour.
She's been training for the marathon.

Usage

Started in the past and is continuing now. Usually takes **for** or **since**.	I have been working for six hours. We've been walking since twelve o'clock.
Lately	I have been feeling much better over the last few days. She has been seeing a new guy recently.
Started in the past and stopped recently. Result is in the present.	What's that smell? Have you been smoking? He's tired. He hasn't been sleeping well.

Usage Note

The difference between the present perfect simple and continuous is what needs to be emphasized.

Present Perfect Simple	Present Perfect Continuous
She's made us a nice cake. result (Now we have a cake.)	I've been eating cake. action (That's what I've been doing.)
I've eaten the whole cake. completion (The cake is gone.)	She's been baking cakes since 1998. length of time (That's a long time.)

Use the simple form with words like **ever** and **never**.

A. Fill in the Blanks

Complete the sentences using the words given. Use the ***present perfect simple*** *or* ***continuous****.*

1. Charlie ________________ (practice) violin all day. He's starting to improve.
2. John ________________ (drink) that beer for an hour. It must be warm now.
3. I ________________ already ________________ (complete) my work. What ________________ you ________________ (do) the whole time?
4. You ________________ (read) that book for weeks. ________________ you ________________ (not finish) it yet?
5. Cindy looks pale today. ________________ she ________________ (catch) a cold?
6. This is the best movie we ________________ ever ________________ (see).

B. Match

Match the two parts.

____	1. Why didn't you call me back?	a.	I think it's a clothing company.
____	2. Has he been annoying you?	b.	Actually, I've never been there.
____	3. Where's Mike?	c.	It's been raining.
____	4. Who has Gina been working for?	d.	Yes. It's great, isn't it?
____	5. Have you tried the wine?	e.	I haven't seen him all day.
____	6. Why is the car all wet?	f.	No. It's been too cold.
____	7. Have you been outside this week?	g.	No. He's always very careful.
____	8. What's your favorite city in Europe?	h.	Sorry. I have been really busy.
____	9. Hey! When did you get here?	i.	I've been sitting behind you the whole time.
____	10. Has he ever broken any bones?	j.	Not at all. He's a nice guy.

C. Correct the Mistakes

Fix the errors in the passage.

Computer sales have never ~~being~~ been higher. Over 300 million computers are now sold every year. Why? More people have surf the Internet. A recent survey shows that people having been using computers more and more for online entertainment. The Internet has been changed home life in a big way. With faster speeds, it can be used for watching television and movies. Many national networks have been put popular programs on their websites. Internet-ready TVs have selling well for the last year. So, for anyone who hasn't have enough choices, get ready for more!

Reading

Before You Read *Discuss the following questions with a partner:*

1. What kind of TV shows do you watch?
2. Do you think TV affects the way people behave?

The Unexpected Effects of Television

Track 29

People often worry about the effects of children watching too much television, but TV doesn't just affect children. Studies have shown that television can influence everyone in many ways.

Shows about the legal system and law enforcement have grown in popularity. Many people think these shows affect the way jurors see the courtroom. Lawyers once blamed the legal drama *Perry Mason* for influencing juries and making them hesitate to find a person guilty. The show would feature a surprising twist when people made dramatic admissions of guilt in the courtroom. Therefore, some lawyers believed juries expected this to happen in real life. Today, some people blame the crime show *CSI* for influencing juries. In *CSI*, evidence from a laboratory is always reliable, so it is thought that juries place a lot of trust in certain kinds of evidence. This is called the "CSI Effect."

Shows about hospitals can also change the way people think. Doctors say that some patients like to guess why they are sick after watching TV shows like *ER*. Usually, these guesses are wrong, but every so often they are correct. One woman, Alexandria Ostrem, began having trouble walking and was able to recognize her rare disease because it was featured on the drama *House*.

There are many other ways television affects people's behavior. Are you aware of what you watch and how it affects you? Your television habits could be changing you in unexpected ways.

A. Synonyms

Match the word or phrase in bold with its synonym.

worry •	• exciting
affect •	• fault
dramatic •	• unusual
guilt •	• know of
rare •	• influence
be aware of •	• be concerned about
guess •	• predict

B. Word Definitions

Use the clues to fill in the blanks with the word choices given. Change the word form if necessary.

blame	jury	hesitate	patient
admission	evidence	reliable	unexpected

1. There is no ______________ that he stole those items. I think he's innocent. (proof)
2. He ______________ the broken alarm clock for making him late. (think something is responsible)
3. You must act quickly and not ______________. (delay)
4. The ______________ determined that the man did not kill his wife. (deciding group)
5. The doctors in this hospital treat their ______________ with respect. (person receiving medical care)
6. News of their divorce was ______________. I didn't think they would ever separate. (surprising)
7. The man made a(n) ______________ of his wrongdoing in the courtroom. (confession)
8. My watch is very ______________ and is never wrong. (can be trusted)

C. Multiple Choice

Circle the correct answers.

1. According to some lawyers, what did viewers of *Perry Mason* expect guilty people to do?
   a. confess to the crime
   b. lie to people
   c. blame others
   d. tell stories

2. Which show(s) is / are blamed for making juries rely heavily on laboratory evidence?
   a. *Perry Mason*
   b. *House* and *ER*
   c. *CSI*
   d. all of the above

3. How can shows like *ER* affect someone's behavior?
   a. They will no longer trust the legal system.
   b. They may try to guess why they're sick.
   c. They may be more likely to work as doctors.
   d. They will get into more trouble in the hospital.

4. What did Alexandria Ostrem do after watching the TV show *House*?
   a. She saved someone else's life.
   b. She caught a criminal outside of her laboratory.
   c. She improved in her ability to write dramas.
   d. She correctly guessed her own disease.

UNIT 8

Music to Our Ears

Have you ever gotten a song stuck in your hea
days? That's just one example of the power of mu
can also make you feel excited, help you through t
times, and even fight an illness.

Words & Expressions

Task I *Listen and use the words given to fill in the blanks in the posters.* Track 30

program	Conductor	tour	Symphony
reserve	Drums	sell out	performance

The Red Hot Chili Peppers are on ❶ ____________.
This legendary rock band will give one ❷ ____________ only!

All band members and new guests

Lead singer: **Anthony Kiedis**
Lead guitar: **Josh Klinghoffer**
Bass guitar: **Michael "Flea" Balzary**
❸ ____________: **Chad Smith**

Tickets will ❹ ____________!
Hurry and buy your ticket today!

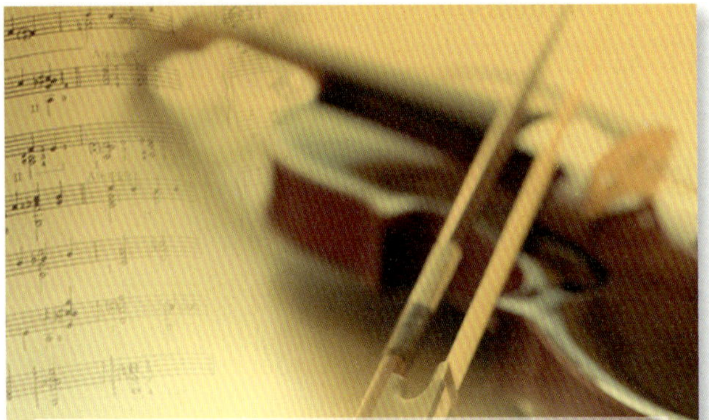

The London ❺ ____________ Orchestra is coming!

❻ ____________: **Daniel Harding**
Violinist: **Janine Jansen**

The ❼ ____________ will include pieces by A. Vivaldi and J. S. Bach.
To ❽ ____________ your seat or get more information, call 1800-555-335.

Task II *Use the correct form of the words given to complete the sentences.*

legendary	performance	lead	concert	sell out
symphony	orchestra	conductor	violinist	

1. My cousin plays the flute in a(n) ____________.
2. The Rolling Stones are a(n) ____________ rock band.
3. You play the violin very well! You should become a professional ____________.
4. A(n) ____________ has to direct and guide many musicians at the same time.
5. In my opinion, Bach wrote the best ____________ ever.
6. We should buy our tickets early. They might ____________.
7. Maggie has a beautiful voice. She's the ____________ singer in a band.
8. Would you like to come to a hip-hop ____________ with me on Friday night?
9. This is the band's last ____________ together.

Listen Up

*Listen and check **True** or **False**.* Track 31

	True	False
1. Elvis Costello made 13 albums before *The Juliet Letters.*	☐	☐
2. The Brodsky Quartet is a rock band.	☐	☐
3. Elvis Costello is a member of the Brodsky Quartet.	☐	☐
4. Elvis Costello wrote the music by himself.	☐	☐
5. The album became available in stores in 1993.	☐	☐
6. This album sounded different than other rock albums.	☐	☐

Language Tip

When we talk about musicians, we often use words that end in the following ways:

Word Ending	Meaning	Example
– ist	a person who plays a certain thing	A **violinist** plays the violin.
– er / – or	a person who performs an action	A **singer** sings.

*Fill in the blanks with **–ist**, **–er**, or **–or**.*

1. A pian______ plays the piano.
2. A compos______ composes music.
3. A conduct______ conducts the orchestra.
4. A drumm______ plays the drums.
5. A guitar______ plays the guitar.

Class Interview

*Find a classmate who answers **yes** to the following questions. Write their name on the chart.*

Do you ...	Classmate
1. have a friend who plays the drums?	______________
2. sing well?	______________
3. enjoy going to the symphony?	______________
4. play the guitar?	______________
5. know someone who composes music?	______________

Match the expressions above with those below and write the student's name.

Statement

1. ____________ knows a songwriter.
2. ____________ likes classical music.
3. ____________ sings in key.
4. ____________ has a drummer friend.
5. ____________ is a guitarist.

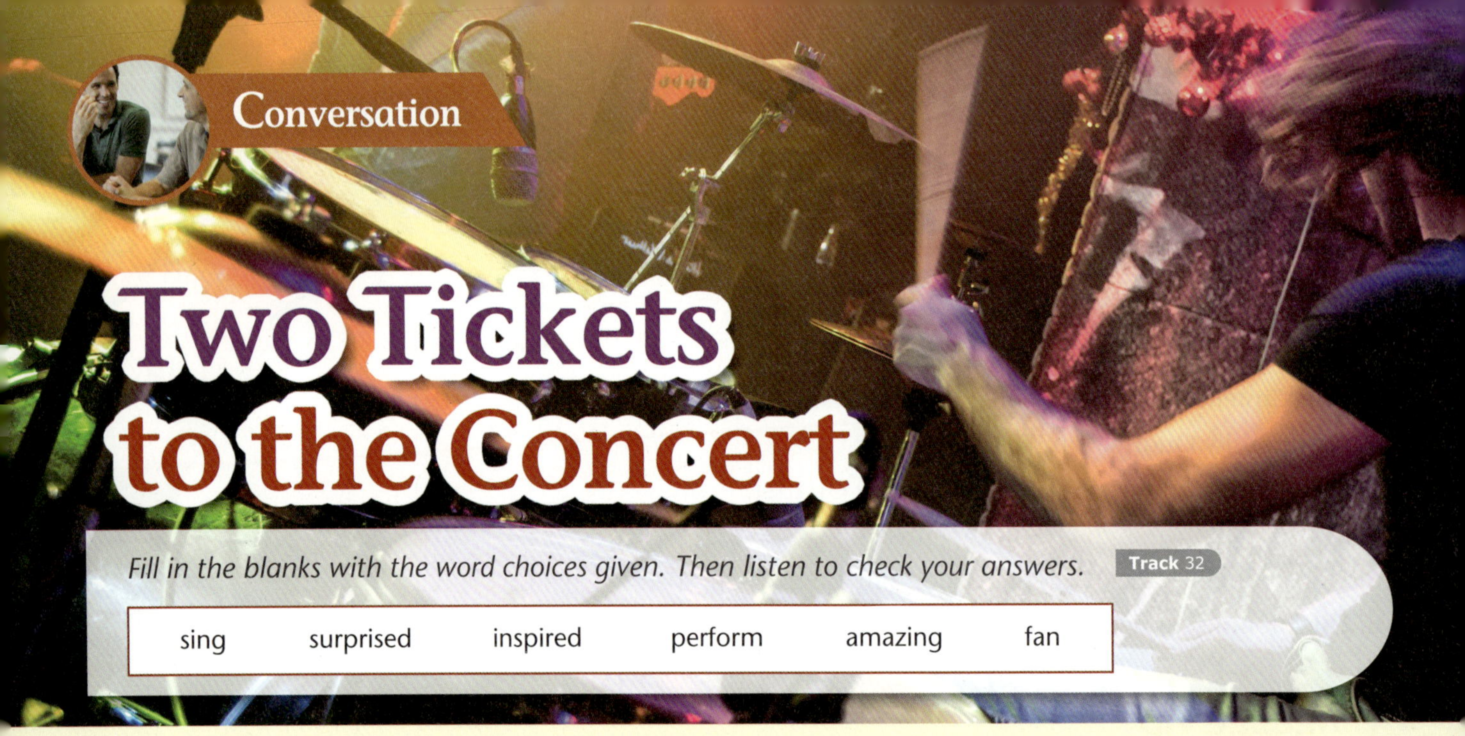

Conversation

Two Tickets to the Concert

Fill in the blanks with the word choices given. Then listen to check your answers. Track 32

sing	surprised	inspired	perform	amazing	fan

Jeff and Eric are buying tickets to a jazz concert.

Jeff: Eric, how's it going? You're going to Pat Metheny's performance too?

Eric: Yes. I love Pat Metheny. He **1.** __________ me to play the guitar. He's an outstanding musician and my role model.

Jeff: I'm also a(n) **2.** __________. I had no idea that you're a guitarist. Do you play in a band?

Eric: Yeah. I started a rock band with some friends. We're not a huge success, but we perform here and there.

Jeff: Cool. I play the drums. Do you need a drummer, by any chance?

Eric: I'm sorry, Jeff. We've already got one. We are looking for a backup singer. Can you sing?

Jeff: Nah. I can't really **3.** __________ in key. Not many people who play the drums are great singers.

Eric: That's too bad.

Jeff: Well, if you learn about a band that needs a drummer, let me know. I'd love to **4.** __________ more.

Eric: Sure thing. Wow, so many people are in line!

Jeff: I'm **5.** __________. I didn't know Pat Metheny was a household name.

Eric: Luckily, we got here ahead of time! Now I'll get to see Pat Metheny, who influenced me so much, playing live.

Jeff: It's going to be a(n) **6.** __________ evening!

A. Word Definitions

Use the clues to fill in the blanks with the word choices given. Change the word form if necessary.

inspire	outstanding	role model	success
in key	in line	influence	live

1. The concert will be broadcast ______________ on television. (not recorded)
2. This restaurant is ______________! It has the best pasta in town. (great)
3. He doesn't sing ______________, but he still sounds OK. He has a nice, deep voice. (properly)
4. We waited ______________ at the bank for 30 minutes. That's why we are late. (row of people)
5. Michelle Obama is a(n) ______________ for people all over America. Young girls especially look up to her. (hero)
6. The woman's tiny store has grown into a huge ______________. (something well-known)
7. Alfred Hitchcock ______________ me to become a filmmaker. (motivate)
8. Your friends can greatly ______________ your actions. (affect)

B. Meanings in Context

Choose the meaning of the sentence in the conversation.

1. Do you need a drummer, by any chance?
   a. Do you need a drummer who tries new things?
   b. Is it possible that you need a drummer?

2. We are looking for a backup singer.
   a. We need a singer to stand at the back of the stage.
   b. We want a second singer to sing on some of our songs.

3. I didn't know Pat Metheny was a household name.
   a. The people in this household are also named Metheny.
   b. I'm surprised to see he's so popular.

4. Luckily, we got here ahead of time!
   a. It's a good thing that we came early.
   b. We'll need some luck to be ahead of the times.

C. Expressions

Expressing Singing Ability

Singing Well	Singing Poorly
sing in key	can't sing in key
be a good / great singer	be a poor / terrible singer
have a lovely singing voice	have a terrible voice
sing perfectly in tune	sing out of tune

Complete the following sentences using the expressions above. More than one answer is possible.

1. We're looking for a new lead singer for our band. We want someone who ______________.
2. I don't like Britney Spears. I think she ______________.
3. My sister can't sing. She ______________.
4. Jeremy is a professional singer. He practiced a lot, and now he ______________.

Grammar

Types of Relative Clauses

Usage	Explanation	Example
Restrictive	Restrictive clauses refer to a smaller group. They provide necessary information for the noun before them. Do not use commas in restrictive clauses.	Not many people who play the drums are great singers. If you learn about a band that needs a drummer, let me know.
Nonrestrictive	Nonrestrictive clauses provide more information, but they are not important to the meaning of the sentence. Use commas in nonrestrictive clauses.	Now I'll get to see Pat Metheny, who influenced me so much, playing live. I like *Cats*, which is probably the most popular Broadway show.

Compare the following examples:

Example	Explanation
Joe's brother who is teaching in university lives next to me.	Joe has more than one brother. The speaker is talking about the one who is teaching in university. The clause gives important information and cannot be removed.
Joe's brother, who is teaching in university, lives next to me.	Joe only has one brother. The real point of the sentence is that Joe's brother lives next to the speaker. The clause is not important and can be removed.

Usage Note

1. We usually use **who** or **that** in a restrictive clause and **who** or **which** in a nonrestrictive clause.
   New York, which is the largest city in America, is an interesting place to visit.
   ~~New York, that is the largest city in America, is an interesting place to visit.~~

2. We can remove the relative pronoun in a restrictive clause when it is the object. This isn't done in a nonrestrictive clause.
   The teacher (whom) we're afraid of will teach us on Friday.
   My dad, whom you met yesterday, wants to invite you to our home tonight.
   ~~My dad, you met yesterday, wants to invite you to our home tonight.~~

A. Identify the Clause

*Read the sentences below. Write **R** if the clause is restrictive or **NR** if it's nonrestrictive.*

1. Rafael Nadal, who is a famous tennis player, is playing on TV right now. ______
2. Students who use drugs will be kicked out of school. ______
3. The birds, which have white feathers, are owls. ______
4. Nicole Kidman, who starred in *Rabbit Hole*, is a wonderful actress. ______
5. That house on the corner, whose roof is red, is over 300 years old. ______
6. He is the man that lied to me. ______

B. Combine the Sentences

*Connect the two sentences using a **nonrestrictive relative clause**. For some questions, more than one answer is correct.*

1. We bought a horse for the girl. / The girl is our daughter.
   → ____.
2. The neighbors come from Hong Kong. / They are fighting.
   → The neighbors ____.
3. Anthony fixed his car. / It was damaged in the typhoon.
   → Anthony ____.
4. Burritos have meat, cheese, and vegetables inside. / They are Mexican food.
   → Burritos ____.
5. Willie was late for work today. / The boss is angry at Willie.
   → Willie ____.

C. Correct the Mistakes

Fix the errors in the passage.

Ernest Hemingway, ~~that~~ who is one of the greatest American writers, was born in 1899. His mother who was a musician, wanted him to study music. Hemingway, thought learning the cello was for girls, preferred baseball and fishing. The outdoors was a topic who was important in his stories later. In WWI, Hemingway worked as an ambulance driver. This was an experience, that deeply influenced the young writer. It changed his view about the world and introduced him to France and Spain. They were two countries which he often wrote about them. Hemingway lived a full life which was shown in his books. They're about bullfighting in Spain, hunting in Kenya, and fishing in Cuba. Today, his work is still as popular as ever.

Before You Read

Discuss the following questions with a partner:

1. When do you listen to music?
2. Can you think of a time when music helped you feel better?

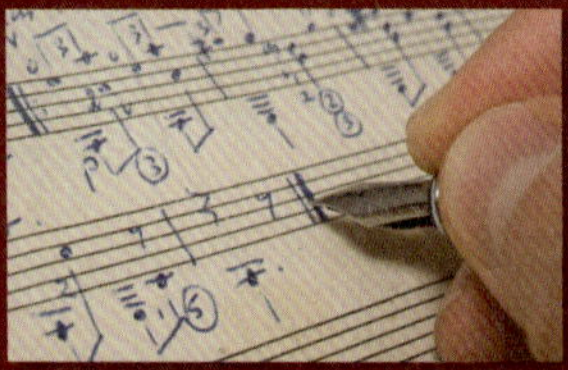

The Healing Power of Music

Track 33

Many people find music to be enjoyable, relaxing, and even therapeutic. In fact, a type of informal music therapy dates back to the first Native Americans and even the ancient Greeks. Native Americans have used music in their healing ceremonies and ancient Greek philosophers believed music could heal not only the body but also the soul. Today, music therapy is widely researched and becoming more formal.

Current studies suggest that music therapy can have vast psychological benefits. In several studies, patients with mental illnesses or disorders, such as depression or dementia, have shown positive results when music was incorporated into their therapies. One impressive example suggested that patients with brain injuries were able to retrain their brains by composing music.

Many people believe that music therapy can also have physical benefits. For instance, researchers have suggested that the relaxing effects of music could reduce the chances of a heart attack in patients with heart disease. Additionally, cancer patients have reported that they have felt less pain when music was a part of their treatment plan.

Studies continue to confirm the benefits of music therapy and find new ways to use music to heal. As researchers continue to discover the advantages of music therapy, we can expect to see it develop into an increasingly formal treatment option.

A. Synonyms

Write the word from the article next to its matching synonym.

1. entertaining: ______ (paragraph 1)	2. sizeable: ______ (paragraph 2)	3. fresh: ______ (paragraph 4)
4. prove: ______ (paragraph 4)	5. unofficial: ______ (paragraph 1)	6. proposed: ______ (paragraph 3)
7. treatment: ______ (paragraph 1)	8. lower: ______ (paragraph 3)	9. cure: ______ (paragraph 1)

B. Word Definitions

Use the clues to fill in the blanks with the word choices given. Change the word form if necessary.

native	ancient	believe	soul
physical	mental	depression	relaxing

1. The ______ humans invented the wheel. (long ago)
2. He is dead, but his ______ lives on. (spirit)
3. When I was in my 20s, I suffered from severe ______. (sadness)
4. Ellen enjoys ______ activities such as reading and napping. (peaceful)
5. He participated in ______ therapy after he injured his knee. (related to the body)
6. Frank thought the exam was a real ______ challenge. He barely passed! (related to the mind)
7. Many people once ______ that the sun revolved around the earth. (accept as true)
8. The ______ people lived on this island long before anyone else. (original)

C. Multiple Choice

Circle the correct answers.

1. How does music help patients with brain injuries?
   a. The sound waves enlarge their brains.
   b. Music really relaxes these patients.
   c. It makes them feel much stronger.
   d. It helps to retrain their brains.

2. Music therapy can benefit cancer patients by helping them to ______.
   a. heal more quickly
   b. develop better hand strength
   c. feel less pain
   d. heal their souls

3. How can music therapy benefit patients with heart disease?
   a. It can successfully cure these patients.
   b. It allows them to stop taking pills.
   c. They are less likely to develop cancer because of music therapy.
   d. It can reduce their chances of getting a heart attack.

4. How long has music therapy been a formal treatment option?
   a. Music therapy is becoming more and more formal today.
   b. People have used formal music therapy since ancient times.
   c. Music therapy is not formally practiced in modern times.
   d. Native Americans were the only professionals who practiced formal music therapy.

UNIT 9

Study Abroad

Going overseas to study can be an eye-opening experie
You learn how to bridge cultural differences, get use
new cuisine, and find your way around a foreign pl
Afterwards, you're ready for anything that comes your w

I Words & Expressions

Task I *Listen and fill in the blanks with the words you hear.* Track 34

process	arrangements	semester	student visa	assistance	effort

Hi Jessie,

It was good to talk to you on the phone. You should definitely study in the United States! The application ❶ ______________ is not very difficult, although it takes a little ❷ ______________. After you select your study topic, you should meet with the study abroad advisor. He or she will make ❸ ______________ for your stay abroad. You also need a(n) ❹ ______________ to study in another country. The advisor can help with this as well. Don't worry about spending an entire ❺ ______________ in a different country. Schools abroad give plenty of ❻ ______________ to foreign students. You might get a bit lonely, but you'll make new friends over time. Here are some of my pictures of New York from last semester. Call me if you need any further help.

Your friend,
Ben

Task II *Complete the crossword using the words from **Task I**. There are some clues below to help you. Don't include spaces between words.*

ACROSS
1. help and support (10)
3. full; complete (6)
5. permission for foreigners to study in a country (7, 4)
7. a large amount of something (6)

DOWN
1. plans and preparation (12)
2. work; energy (6)
4. a series of actions (7)
6. a subject (5)
8. to choose (6)

Listen Up

*Listen and check **True** or **False**.* Track 35

	True	False
1. Mary lived with a French family in Paris.	☐	☐
2. Mary didn't know any French when she went to Paris.	☐	☐
3. Mary missed her family and friends.	☐	☐
4. By the time Mary finished the program, she spoke French well.	☐	☐
5. Overall, the year in Paris was a bad experience for Mary.	☐	☐
6. Mary thinks that studying abroad is not for everyone.	☐	☐

Language Tip

To be or feel **lonely** is to be alone and feel sad because there's no one to talk to.
To be **alone** is to be without others, but it doesn't have to be a bad thing.

*Fill in the blanks with **alone** or **lonely**.*

1. I often go to the movies ____________ on Sundays.
2. I like traveling ____________. I get ____________ sometimes, but it doesn't bother me too much.
3. Mark has very few friends, but he rarely feels ____________.

Class Interview

Talk to your partner. Would they have these problems if they were to study abroad?

	Would Be a Problem	Might Be a Minor Problem	Wouldn't Be a Problem at All
1. Getting used to new surroundings			
2. Feeling homesick			
3. Being able to afford the fees			
4. Experiencing loneliness			
5. Dealing with language barriers			
6. Having to learn independence			
7. Getting over culture shock			

Share your partner's opinions with the class using the expressions below.

learning to live in a new place	missing their home country	paying for studying abroad
feeling lonely	having language problems	handling new customs

My partner thinks that ________________________ could be difficult / could be a small problem / wouldn't be an issue.

Conversation

A Big Decision

Fill in the blanks with the word choices given. Then listen to check your answers. Track 36

complicated	apply	barrier	ideal	thought	homesick

Charles and Lana meet at a coffee shop on campus.

Charles: Hey, Lana. What's new?

Lana: Hey, Charles. I'm thinking about studying abroad next year.

Charles: That's great! Did you start making arrangements?

Lana: I didn't even **1.** __________ yet.

Charles: Is the application process **2.** __________?

Lana: No. It's pretty painless, but I can't choose the country where I want to go.

Charles: How do you feel about Spain?

Lana: I'd love to experience Spanish culture firsthand; however, I don't speak Spanish. I'm worried about feeling lonely and **3.** __________.

Charles: The language **4.** __________ could be an obstacle. How about England?

Lana: There are several reasons why I don't like England; for example, the weather there is horrible.

Charles: Then Australia would be **5.** __________. It's warm, and getting a student visa for Australia is a breeze. Besides, Australians are welcoming people.

Lana: I'm concerned about sunburns. The sun is very strong in Australia.

Charles: That's true.

Lana: Maybe I shouldn't go. I have many friends here. Also, the weather is always nice.

Charles: Don't be scared of challenges. Of course living overseas is no walk in the park, but you'll adjust. Why don't you sleep on it before you decide?

Lana: You're right. I'll give it some more **6.** __________.

A. Word Definitions

Use the clues to fill in the blanks with the word choices given.

apply complicated obstacle horrible ideal welcoming adjust

1. The family I stayed with in Seattle was very ____________. (generous to visitors)
2. My paper is ____________. I will definitely get a bad grade. (awful)
3. New Zealand is the ____________ place to take a vacation. It's beautiful, clean, and safe. (perfect)
4. The computer program is too ____________. I can't understand it. (complex)
5. I want to be a basketball star, but my height is a(n) ____________. (barrier)
6. I am writing to ____________ for the position advertised on your website. (request)
7. Tommy is trying to ____________ to a new school environment. (become used to)

B. Meanings in Context

Choose the meaning of the sentence in the conversation.

1. It's pretty painless.
   - a. It hurts. But it doesn't hurt a lot.
   - b. It's not going to cause you too much trouble.
2. I'd love to experience Spanish culture firsthand.
   - a. I want to see the culture for myself.
   - b. The culture was the first I experienced.
3. Getting a student visa for Australia is a breeze.
   - a. It's difficult to get a student visa.
   - b. Getting a student visa is easy.
4. Don't be scared of challenges.
   - a. Try new things sometimes.
   - b. If a challenge comes up, run away.
5. Living overseas is no walk in the park, but you'll adjust.
   - a. Lots of countries don't have parks, but you'll adapt.
   - b. Living in a new country isn't easy, but you'll get used to it.
6. Why don't you sleep on it before you decide?
   - a. You look tired. Decide and then take a rest.
   - b. Don't make a decision now.

C. Expressions

Thinking about Decisions

sleep on (*something*)	give (*something*) some thought
think (*something*) over / through	think about / consider (*something*) carefully
don't rush / jump into (*something*)	

Use the expressions above in the blanks. Practice saying the lines with a partner.

1. **A:** I'm planning to break up with Patrick. **B:** Are you sure? ____________.
2. **A:** Do you think I should quit my job? **B:** I don't know. ____________.
3. **A:** I can't decide on the topic of my essay. **B:** That's a big decision. ____________.

Grammar

Adverbs

Relative Adverbs

Relative adverbs, such as **where**, **when**, and **why**, come before a relative clause.

Adverb Pattern	Example
where (preposition + which)	I can't choose the country where (to which) I want to go.
when (preposition + which)	She was born on a day when (on which) her father was out of town.
why (for which)	There are several reasons why (for which) I don't like England.

Usage Note

We can leave out the relative adverb in some clauses. Writers often prefer **that** to **why** in a clause referring to **reason**.
Dick looks forward to the day **(when)** he doesn't have to go to school.
Do you know the reason **(why)** Holly doesn't like poetry?
I know the reason **(that)** my wife likes to shop.

Conjunctive Adverbs

Conjunctive adverbs are usually used to join ideas.

Function	Adverb	Example
Contrast	however, instead, otherwise, on the other hand	I'd love to experience Spanish culture firsthand; **however**, I don't speak Spanish.
Give an example	for example, for instance	There are several reasons why I don't like England; **for example**, the weather there is horrible.
Add information	besides, also, in addition	**Besides**, Australians are welcoming people. **Also**, the weather is always nice.
Provide emphasis	of course, in fact, indeed	**Of course** living overseas is no walk in the park, but you'll adjust.

Usage Note

Pay attention to the punctuation:
I didn't go to the carnival. **Instead**, I went hiking with my friend.
I didn't go to the carnival; **instead**, I went hiking with my friend.
I didn't go to the carnival. I went hiking with my friend **instead**.

A. Combine the Sentences

*Connect the two sentences using **where, when**, or **why**.*

1. I'm looking forward to next Wednesday. / My holiday starts then.
   → I'm ____.
2. Terry works in a building. / The building is located in New York.
   → The building ____.
3. You don't want to go to Southern University. / Please tell me the reason.
   → Please tell ____.
4. Do you remember the day? / On that day, we went camping.
   → Do you ____?
5. I grew up on a farm. / There were many cows and sheep on the farm.
   → I grew ______________________ ______________________.

B. Fill in the Blanks

Use the word choices given to complete the sentences. Add commas if necessary.

however	instead	for example	in addition	of course	in fact

1. Leo doesn't go to baseball games. He watches them on TV ____________.
2. Roger likes different kinds of ice cream; ____________ he enjoys mango, vanilla, and chocolate.
3. Lance is a good athlete and is still in amazing shape. ____________ he ran in the Boston Marathon last year.
4. Pam normally goes to the Philippines during the Lunar New Year holiday; ____________ she is visiting her aunt in Hawaii this year.
5. We don't start work until nine; you're free to come early ____________.
6. Jerry is a friendly guy; ____________ he's extremely generous.

C. Correct the Mistakes

Fix the errors in the passage.

Most people know that foods with fiber are good for you because they help your digestion. Addition, they help you to develop a strong heart. ~~Beside~~ Besides improving digestion and heart health, they are also low in fat. However, most people do not know that fiber has even more benefits. Foods rich in fiber, such as beans and oranges, also help you to live longer. According to research, if you're over 50 years old and eat 30 grams of fiber a day, you lower your chances of dying from certain diseases by 22 percent. On another hand, people who do not eat many foods that are rich in fiber are not likely to live so long. For example, a hamburger and fries may taste better than broccoli and cereal, but researchers can give reasons why you shouldn't eat these kinds of foods. In indeed, researchers can give many reasons why foods rich in fiber are better for you.

Before You Read

Discuss the following questions with a partner:

1. Where would you like to go if you had the opportunity to study abroad?
2. How might studying abroad help you in your studies?

Adventures Abroad

Track 37

Studying abroad is an exciting opportunity for students to encounter new cultures and experiences. While many study abroad applicants go to Europe and the United States, they also have the option to explore other unfamiliar and less-frequented places.

Some study abroad programs can take students to very remote countries. One such program sends students to Irkutsk in Russia. Irkutsk is one of the largest cities in the frozen Siberian region of Russia. By 1900, it had earned the nickname "The Paris of Siberia." It is a great place to practice Russian and learn Russian history. For a truly remote experience, it's hard to get farther away from civilization than McMurdo Station, Antarctica. A typical program there lets students survey the coldest place on the planet while they help scientists make discoveries about climate change and the environment.

For a warmer destination, students may want to study near the blue waters of the Maldives. These islands are surrounded by various aquatic life, which makes them a popular destination for marine biology students. They are also said to be among the most beautiful locations on earth.

When choosing where to study abroad, applicants should consider more than a destination's popularity. They should also think about all that they will learn. Regardless of which destination a student chooses, studying abroad will help them to discover something new about other cultures and themselves.

A. Synonyms

Write the word from the article next to its matching synonym.

1. find: ______________ (paragraph 4)	2. thrilling: ______________ (paragraph 1)	3. attractive: ______________ (paragraph 3)
4. faraway: ______________ (paragraph 2)	5. travel: ______________ (paragraph 1)	6. unknown: ______________ (paragraph 1)
7. normal: ______________ (paragraph 2)	8. meet: ______________ (paragraph 1)	9. weather: ______________ (paragraph 2)

B. Word Definitions

Use the clues to fill in the blanks with the word choices given. Change the word form if necessary.

adventure	applicant	locate	frozen
civilization	survey	destination	surround

1. The new factory will be ______________ in Minsk. (situate)
2. That hike into the jungle was quite a(n) ______________! (exciting journey)
3. The water in this lake is ______________, so we can walk on it. (ice-covered)
4. He is driving to his ______________. (journey's end)
5. When we get back to ______________, I'm going to take a hot shower. (modern life)
6. We have four ______________ who want the job. (candidate)
7. Robots help scientists ______________ the surface of the moon. (inspect)
8. The ocean ______________ the island. (enclose)

C. Multiple Choice

Circle the correct answers.

1. Where is Irkutsk?
   a. Siberia
   b. Mali
   c. Africa
   d. Antarctica

2. What are students likely to study in Irkutsk?
   a. the Russian language
   b. something in a computer lab
   c. something about animals
   d. how people behave

3. Which of the following is correct?
   a. McMurdo Station, Antarctica, is usually a very crowded place.
   b. The weather conditions at McMurdo Station are pretty normal.
   c. Students and scientists cannot work together at McMurdo Station.
   d. Scientists are trying to understand the environment at McMurdo Station.

4. How are the Maldives described?
   a. They are surrounded by clear blue water and lots of marine life.
   b. They are very cold, and there are few people around.
   c. Many people live there, and the water is unclean.
   d. They are located in Russia.

UNIT 10

Technology and You

No matter who you are, technology influences you Some people rely on the Internet for almost every they do. Others do not care for computers but still li watch TV, use a microwave oven, and so on. Techn is all around us, and it's constantly changing.

Words & Expressions

Task I *Listen and fill in the blanks.* Track 38

development	behind the times	technical	delete	digital	darkrooms	capacity

FILM IS HISTORY; DIGITAL CAMERAS ARE THE FUTURE

Has ❶ ______________ photography killed film? Cameras all used film until the 1990s. Photography was difficult and ❷ ______________. Photo journalists often used ❸ ______________ to produce their own pictures. After the ❹ ______________ of digital cameras, the world became a different place. Now, people can just take a picture and see what it looks like right away. The cameras have a huge ❺ ______________. They can hold thousands of pictures. If you don't like them, you can just ❻ ______________ them. You can also easily put them on your computer or online. Many companies have even stopped making film cameras. It looks like using film is ❼ ______________, and digital technology is in.

Task II *Choose the answers.*

1. I got a new **digital** camera. I can take pictures without using film / lenses.
2. I really love **photography**. Taking pictures / Recording music is great fun.
3. I'm out of **film**. I can't send / take any more pictures.
4. Jim has a lot of **technical** knowledge. He is good with machines / languages.
5. I'm studying the **development** of plants. I want to know how they live / grow.
6. The theater has a low **capacity**. It only has a small number of seats / actors.
7. I **deleted** the file. It was removed from / stored in my computer.
8. That style is **behind the times**. Nobody / Everybody wears it today.
9. **Technology** is a big part of our lives. How could we live without food / computers?
10. That movie seems to be **in** right now. Lots of people like it / are bored of it.

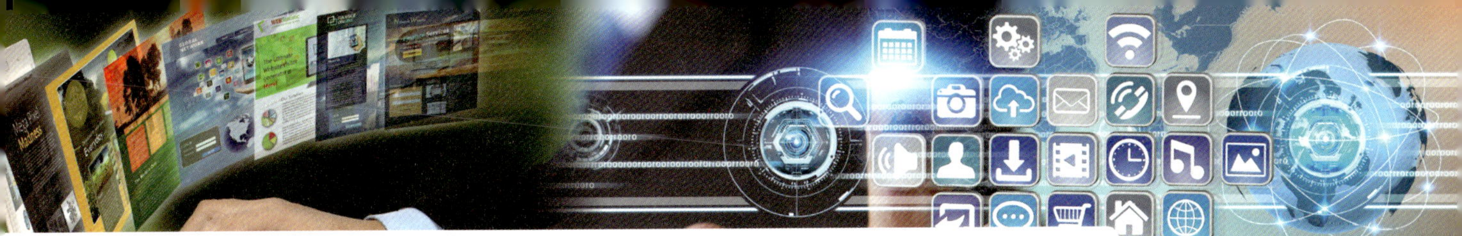

Listen Up

*Listen and check **True** or **False**.* Track 39

	True	False
1. Alice really likes the new teacher.	☐	☐
2. Jeremy is interested in using computers for art.	☐	☐
3. They both think that learning about computers takes too much time.	☐	☐
4. Alice needs to buy a new computer.	☐	☐
5. The new computer programs are more difficult than before.	☐	☐
6. Jeremy will teach Alice some of the easiest functions.	☐	☐

Language Tip

*The word **application** has a number of meanings. Match the sentence to the definition.*

____ 1. Most phone **applications** are games.

____ 2. My **application** to the university was accepted.

____ 3. Plastic has many **applications**. We can make bags, bottles, and clothes from it.

a. a written request
b. a practical use
c. a piece of computer software

Class Interview

Work with your partner. Write the word next to its definition.

quality	state-of-the-art	applications	fancy	handy	convenience	practical

1. (*n.*) games and other software: ____________
2. (*adj.*) easy to use: ____________
3. (*adj.*) looks good: ____________
4. (*adj.*) useful in everyday life: ____________
5. (*n.*) being easy / saving time: ____________
6. (*adj.*) the most modern: ____________
7. (*n.*) how good or bad: ____________

Ask your partner the following questions. Then share the results with the class.

1. When you're buying electronics, is quality or price more important?
2. What's the best piece of electronics that you own? Is it fancy or practical?
3. Which cell phone is the most state-of-the-art? Talk about its functions.
4. Does your cell phone have any cool applications?
5. How important is convenience to you? Do you buy online or in a store?
6. What's the handiest invention ever? The computer? The microwave?

Conversation

Making the Right Choice

Fill in the blanks with the word choices given. Then listen to check your answers. Track 40

illegal	quality	secondhand	regular	deals	handy

Kyle and Tom are looking at iPhones.

Kyle: I can't believe you want a fake iPhone.

Tom: My girlfriend told me to get one because they were **1.** __________.

Kyle: A newspaper article said that fake products were worthless. It also warned that they might be of poor **2.** __________.

Tom: Yeah, but real ones don't come cheap. My brother said that the fake iPhones in this store were state-of-the-art. They have all the applications of **3.** __________ iPhones.

Kyle: If you want convenience, get an iPhone 4. People say they're practical too.

Tom: They're fancy, but they cost an arm and a leg.

Kyle: Then how about a(n) **4.** __________ iPhone? They're a bit behind the times, but they aren't so expensive.

Tom: That's good, but I still think a fake one would come in handy.

Kyle: If you get a piece of junk, you'll be stuck with it! They won't let you return it because they're **5.** __________.

Tom: I think it's worth it. I'll save a lot of money.

Kyle: Why don't we look online for a real one? My classmate told me that you could find some good **6.** __________.

Tom: Alright! I've made up my mind. I'll look for a real iPhone.

Kyle: You won't regret it.

A. Word Definitions

Use the clues to fill in the blanks with the word choices given.

fake	handy	worthless	state-of-the-art	secondhand

1. These tools are ______________. You can use them for all kinds of stuff. (useful)
2. Emily's bag looks fancy, but I think it's ______________. (false)
3. That hospital is very modern. It uses ______________ equipment. (high-tech)
4. If you think a new car is too expensive, you should buy a ______________ one. (used)
5. Why not throw away that old radio? It's completely ______________. (valueless)

B. Meanings in Context

Choose the meaning of the sentence in the conversation.

1. Real ones don't come cheap.
   a. Real ones aren't here yet.
   b. Real ones cost more money.

2. They cost an arm and a leg.
   a. They're quite expensive.
   b. They are extremely dangerous.

3. I still think a fake one would come in handy.
   a. A fake one would be useful.
   b. A fake one would be smaller.

4. I think it's worth it.
   a. I think the value equals the cost.
   b. I think it's worth a lot of money.

5. If you get a piece of junk, you'll be stuck with it!
   a. If you get something useless, you need to throw it away.
   b. If you get something worthless, you won't be able to get rid of it.

6. You won't regret it.
   a. You will be confused about the decision.
   b. You will be happy with your decision.

C. Expressions

Expressing Function

Useful	Useless
be handy	be worthless
be practical	be of poor quality
come in handy	be a piece of junk / garbage
be of use	be a lemon (for cars)

Fill in the blanks using the expressions above. Each blank has more than one correct choice.

1. Don't get that cell phone. It's ______________.
2. This flashlight may ______________ in a dark cave.
3. Henry's car is ______________. If he tries to sell it, he won't get any money.

Grammar

Reported Speech

Requests / Orders

	Direct Speech	Reported Speech
Affirmative	My girlfriend: "Get a fake iPhone."	My girlfriend **told me to get** a fake iPhone.
Negative	My girlfriend: "Don't get a fake iPhone."	My girlfriend **told me not to get** a fake iPhone.

Questions

When you change a regular question into reported speech, follow the statement word order: **subject** + **verb**.

	Direct Speech	Reported Speech
Yes / No Questions	Nick: "Do you speak Japanese?"	Nick asked me **whether / if I spoke** Japanese.
Wh- Questions	Nick: "Why do you study Japanese?"	Nick asked me **why I studied** Japanese.

Statements

If the sentence starts in the present, the tense does not change in reported speech. If the sentence starts in the past, the tense needs to change.

From	To
Simple Present	Simple Present
People: "iPhones are practical."	People **say** iPhones are practical.
Simple Present	Simple Past
An article: "Fake products are worthless."	An article **said** that fake products were worthless.
will / may / can	would / might / could
An article: "They may be of poor quality."	An article **warned** that they might be of poor quality.
My classmate: "You can find some good deals online."	My classmate **told** me that I could find some good deals online.

Usage Note

Modals like **could**, **might**, **would**, or **should** usually don't change in reported speech.

Direct Speech: Andrew: "I **should** clean my room."

Reported Speech: Andrew **said** that he **should** clean his room.

A. Fill in the Blanks

Complete the sentences to make ***reported requests****.*

1. "Hurry up and finish your homework."
   → The teacher told me ______________________________.
2. "Please be on time tomorrow."
   → My brother asked me ______________________________.
3. "Give me your opinion."
   → The boss asked Michael ______________________________.
4. "Don't forget your camera."
   → Debby reminded me ______________________________.
5. "Make sure to study for the test."
   → My mother told me ______________________________.

B. Rewrite the Sentences

Change the sentences into ***reported speech****.*

1. "I won't be late," said Stephen.
   → ____.
2. "I want to try the pasta," said Ryan.
   → ____.
3. "I don't understand you," said Kate.
   → ____.
4. "My son speaks German very well," says Judy.
   → ____.
5. "You should keep practicing," said Ken.
   → ____.

C. Correct the Mistakes

Fix the errors in the passage.

I've always wanted to try skydiving. My friend told me not [to] do it because it was dangerous. My cousin also say that it was too scary. I don't care! I want to make up my own mind. I read an article that said you can try skydiving in lots of different places. It also mentioned that the first time you try it, you have to jump with a teacher. It is much safer that way, the article said. I asked my brother does he want to try it with me, but he said he not want to. He said that it be too risky! He told me that he likes skiing and skating, but he won't jump out of an airplane. I guess I'll have to find someone else who is willing to try something new.

Reading

Before You Read *Discuss the following questions with a partner:*

1. How has technology changed your life?
2. What are your predictions about technology in the future?

Robots Today and Tomorrow

Track 41

Until recently, the idea of robots taking over household chores seemed like a figment of our imaginations. It would have been hard to imagine robots vacuuming or mopping our floors, let alone performing more sophisticated tasks. However, analysts believe that robots will continue to advance and become an important part of our everyday lives.

We might be unaware of how many robots are either already in our houses or are available on the market. Many people already know the household robots from the company iRobot, which vacuum, mop, and even clean gutters. However, most people are probably unfamiliar with Kiva robots and the uBOT-5. Kiva robots, which lift heavy objects and help workers in Amazon's warehouses, improve Amazon's packing and shipping efficiency. The uBot-5, which has yet to be mass produced, was designed to help the elderly. It can perform tasks such as taking vitals, reminding someone to take medication, and even sending an alert for emergency services.

While the field of robotics has shown impressive advancements, robots currently do not possess the ability to have or understand emotions. However, robotics experts are currently attempting to design robots that can recognize expressions and communicate with humans. Some experts predict that robots will be able to truly think and feel in the near future. Robots may eventually be smarter than we are!

A. Synonyms

Write the word from the article next to its matching synonym.

1. unconscious: ______ (paragraph 2)	2. feelings: ______ (paragraph 3)	3. alarm: ______ (paragraph 2)
4. advanced: ______ (paragraph 1)	5. foresee: ______ (paragraph 3)	6. existing: ______ (paragraph 2)
7. talk: ______ (paragraph 3)	8. senior citizens: ______ (paragraph 2)	9. home: ______ (paragraph 1)

B. Word Definitions

Use the clues to fill in the blanks with the word choices given.

possess	analyst	important	emergency	expression

1. My family is a(n) ______ part of my life. (essential)
2. Her father was a computer ______. He knew about many different computer programs. (expert who predicts)
3. John does not ______ the skills to complete this task. (own or have)
4. I knew something was wrong as soon as I saw his ______. (the look on one's face)
5. The car accident is a(n) ______ situation. An ambulance is coming. (crisis)

C. Words with Different Meanings

Match the word in bold with its definition.

1
The invention of the wheel was an important **advance** in human history. ______
This new computer has the most **advanced** technology. ______
Definition: ⓐ *adj.* modern ⓑ *n.* development

2
In college, she studied **performing** arts. ______
We watched the dog **perform** many different tricks. ______
Definition: ⓐ *v.* to demonstrate ⓑ *adj.* related to drama

3
The mother **recognized** the cry of her child. ______
The soldier was **recognized** for his bravery with a medal. ______
Definition: ⓐ *v.* to be familiar with something ⓑ *adj.* publicly honored

D. True or False

*Check **True** or **False**.*

	True	False
1. Experts have not created any robots that can clean our houses.	☐	☐
2. Robots that can completely understand our language exist today.	☐	☐
3. The uBOT-5 was designed to take care of the elderly.	☐	☐
4. Experts are trying to create robots that can identify people's emotions.	☐	☐
5. Scientists do not believe robots will ever be able to think and feel.	☐	☐

UNIT 11

Right and Wrong

Not everyone agrees on what is right and wh
wrong. Have you ever done anything that seemec
to you but wrong to your friends? In your opir
what are the most important rules in life?

I Words & Expressions

Task I *Listen and fill in the blanks.* Track 42

copying	worry	stop	professor	fault	cheating

Dear Anne,

I'm writing because I don't know what to do. I saw a student in my literature class ❶ ___________ on an exam. He wrote down quotes on a piece of paper and was ❷ ___________ them. I didn't say anything to the ❸ ___________, but now I wonder if I should inform him. Cheating is wrong, but the student could be suspended.

C. M.

Dear C.M.,

The cheater is guilty. You shouldn't ❹ ___________ about the penalty. That's his ❺ ___________. Remember that you don't have any evidence. Without that, the professor can't do anything. I think you should talk to the cheater and tell him to ❻ ___________. If he does it again, tell the teacher.

Anne

Task II *Complete the crossword using the words from* ***Task I****. There are some clues below to help you.*

ACROSS
1. doing something wrong (6)
3. this shows that something is true (8)
4. a punishment (7)
5. to put someone out of school for a short time (7)
6. to tell (6)

DOWN
2. books, plays, or poems (10)
4. a person who teaches in university (9)

Listen Up

Listen and complete the sentences with the words you hear. Track 43

1. The speaker heard a(n) ______________. A girl in her class was ______________ and selling CDs.
2. The girl was selling ______________ outside the ______________.
3. She thought that her ______________ was bad for the school's ______________.
4. They were ______________ by the police and got ______________.
5. She is ______________ to explain to her ______________ tomorrow.

Language Tip

A **fine** is money you need to pay for breaking a law. A **penalty** is a loss for breaking a rule. **Punishment** is a general word for what happens when you do something wrong.

Fill in the blanks with the appropriate words. Sometimes more than one choice is possible.

1. I parked my car in the wrong place. I had to pay a huge ______________.
2. Some countries will cut off your hand as a ______________ for stealing.
3. I don't think that physical ______________ is good for children.

Class Interview

Work with a partner. Take turns asking about the situations.

1. Your friend keeps copying your homework. She could get you both suspended. Will you **take the risk** and help her again?

2. Someone is spreading **rumors** about a girl in Mark's class. Mark doesn't like the girl, but the stories are not true. What should he do?

3. Your classmate always has the best movies. He says he **pirates** them. Will you go to his house to watch some?

4. Julia's report is **due** tomorrow. She has a great **reputation**, so nobody would check if she stole it from the Internet. What should she do?

Write the word or phrase in bold next to its definition. Compare your answers to your partner's.

1. expected: ______________
2. to do something dangerous: ______________
3. to illegally copy something: ______________
4. news that might be true: ______________
5. how people think of you: ______________

Conversation

Caught on the WEB

Fill in the blanks with the word choices given. Then listen to check your answers. Track 44

or	comments	suspended	careful	guilty	papers

Nicole and Joe are studying together in the library.

Nicole: Let's take a break. I'm tired out. Hey, did you hear about that student who got suspended?

Joe: No. What happened?

Nicole: I hear that he posted **1.** __________ online.

Joe: What did he write?

Nicole: He wrote that one of the professors was copying from others' academic **2.** __________.

Joe: How did people find out about the comments?

Nicole: Either the professor **3.** __________ his students often visit the website.

Joe: That student took a risk. Maybe he got burned-out and blamed his teacher. I wonder when he'll be able to return to school.

Nicole: Word is that he was **4.** __________ for six weeks. The professor is very angry. He's taking the student to court!

Joe: Six weeks is a long time. Students should be **5.** __________ about posting online. People's reputations are important. If someone spreads rumors about me, I'm going to lose my cool too.

Nicole: Yeah. It isn't moral. You need evidence. Otherwise, you might be found **6.** __________ in court.

Joe: The teaching staff is in a meeting about this issue. What will the teachers do?

Nicole: I don't know. But he is a law professor. The student messed with the wrong guy!

A. Word Definitions

Use the clues to fill in the blanks with the word choices given. Change the word form if necessary.

be tired out	post	comment	academic	be able to	otherwise	staff

1. Please keep your ______________ to yourself. Nobody wants to hear what you think. (expressed ideas)
2. After hiking all day, the people in the group ______________. (be exhausted)
3. That school has a great ______________ reputation. (related to education)
4. I won't ______________ go to your home tonight. I have to work. (can)
5. The ______________ at this hotel is very good. We're happy with the service. (workers)
6. Jeff just ______________ a story on his website about his favorite movie. (publish)
7. You'd better take an umbrella. ______________, you're going to get wet. (If not)

B. Meanings in Context

Choose the meaning of the sentence in the conversation.

1. That student took a risk.
   a. That student put himself in danger.
   b. That student was in trouble.

2. He got burned-out and blamed his teacher.
   a. He was tired and thought it was his teacher's fault.
   b. He thinks his teacher started the fire.

3. He's taking the student to court!
   a. He'll bring the student in front of a judge.
   b. He'll bring the student to play basketball.

4. If someone spreads rumors about me, I'm going to lose my cool too.
   a. If someone lies about me, it'll make me look bad.
   b. If someone lies about me, I'll get angry.

5. It isn't moral.
   a. You won't make money this way.
   b. It isn't the right thing to do.

6. The student messed with the wrong guy!
   a. It was a mistake to bother him.
   b. The student made a mess in his office.

C. Expressions

Sharing Information

I hear that ...	A little bird told me that ...
Word is that ...	Word on the street is that ...
Rumor has it that ...	

Use the word choices below to practice the expressions above.

Greg and Lindsay are dating	Sam is leaving school
our professor will retire	that shop is going to close down

A: Word on the street is that Greg and Lindsay are dating.

B: That's a little strange. I thought they didn't like each other.

Grammar

Subject and Verb Agreement

In a sentence, the subject and verb must agree: both must be either singular or plural.

Rule 1
If the subjects are joined by **and** or **both** ... **and** ..., they are plural.
Both Martin and his girlfriend **are** running in the park.
Rule 2
If the subjects are joined by **or**, **either** ... **or** ..., or **neither** ... **nor** ..., the verb agrees with the closest subject.
Either the professor or his students often **visit** the website. Either the students or the professor often **visits** the website.
Rule 3
Singular indefinite pronouns use singular verbs. Plural indefinite pronouns use plural verbs. Some pronouns can be singular or plural.
One of the professors **was** copying from others' academic papers. If someone **spreads** rumors about me, I'm going to lose my cool too.
Rule 4
Collective nouns are groups of things. They take a singular verb when the things act together but a plural verb when they act as individuals.
The teaching staff **is** in a meeting about this issue. The teaching staff **disagree** about the issue.
Rule 5
With amounts of money, time, or distance, use a singular verb.
Six weeks **is** a long time. 20 dollars **is** too much for that hat.

Usage Note

When **either** or **neither** is the subject, it always uses a singular verb.

For Example:

Neither of them **is** available to speak right now.

Either of us **is** able to do the job.

A. Choose the Answers

Circle the correct form of the words.

1. Jeff or Devon __________ coffee for us every morning.
   a. make b. makes

2. Neither he nor his brothers __________ the homework assignment.
   a. understand b. understands

3. One of the restaurants on Lake Street __________ open until 11 p.m.
   a. are b. is

4. Baseball players are rich. Some __________ millions every year.
   a. get b. gets

5. The tall man with all the dogs __________ on this trail every day.
   a. walk b. walks

6. Nine miles __________ a long way to go. Maybe we should take a taxi.
   a. are b. is

7. The commercial, which is on many different TV channels, __________ two talking monkeys.
   a. include b. includes

B. Fill in the Blanks

Use the correct form of the words in parentheses to complete the sentences.

1. The group of students __________ (be) nervous about the test tomorrow.
2. The crowd __________ (be) singing the song loudly. I can't even talk with the person next to me!
3. The staff __________ (have) different working habits.
4. There is a protest today. The public __________ (want) a new government.
5. The team __________ (change) clothes after practice every day.

C. Correct the Mistakes

Fix the errors in the passage.

Every February, people around the world ~~watches~~ watch the Super Bowl. The National Football League have 32 teams, and the best two gets to play in the game. It is called a bowl because many football stadiums be shaped like a bowl. Groups of fans celebrates the day by getting together with friends and eating snacks. Either Buffalo wings or pizza are at every Super Bowl party. My favorite team, the Bengals, have never won a Super Bowl game. 40 years are a long time to go without a championship. Both serious and casual fans watch the Super Bowl. A huge crowd are found at most sports bars. The game, which earn millions of dollars, is one of America's biggest traditions. Everyone join in the fun, so you should too!

Reading

Before You Read *Discuss the following questions with a partner:*

1. What are some social issues that you believe are important?
2. Have you ever helped a charity or done volunteer work?

College Students and Charity

Track 45

Although the college years are often considered an occasion for nothing but studying and partying, they can also be a great time for students to learn how to care for society. In recent years, several individual students and organizations have shown how they can make a difference in our world.

Tom Cody, a business student at the University of Connecticut, created adDonations.com. On this website, he sells advertising space and gives the earnings to various charities. Lisa Boragine realized how much waste a typical college student creates when she studied at Syracuse University. Shortly after she graduated, she founded Dump & Run, a charity that collects and resells secondhand items that college students donate.

Some of the biggest annual college charity events are planned by student organizations. In 2002, UCLA students planned the AXE Undie Run Challenge, an event where runners took off their clothes and ran in their underwear. The runners' clothes were donated to charity. Today, many other schools also participate in this race, and tens of thousands of dollars' worth of clothing are given to the homeless.

Another popular student event is Penn State's dance marathon — THON. At this event, students dance throughout the entire night without sitting or sleeping to collect money. The money is then donated to the Four Diamonds Fund, which helps support children who are battling cancer. In 1973, THON raised several thousands of dollars, but in 2010, the students collected almost eight million dollars. Now, it is the largest student charity event in the world.

Students have raised money for the needy in remarkable ways. These efforts show that college students are capable of more than just helping themselves. They are also capable of helping many others throughout our society.

A. Word Definitions

Use the clues to fill in the blanks with the word choices given. Change the word form if necessary.

various	annual	donate	marathon	needy	remarkable	capable

1. Ants are ______________ of digging complicated tunnel systems. (able to do something)
2. Nancy cares about the earth. She ______________ to an environmental organization each month. (give money to)
3. We are going to host an all-day movie ______________. We will watch movies from morning until late at night. (long event)
4. The Edinburgh Festival is a(n) ______________ event, which takes place in the summer. (yearly)
5. Leonardo da Vinci was a(n) ______________ painter and inventor. (extraordinary)
6. Sally spends her weekends serving food to the ______________. (poor)
7. People from ______________ countries, such as France and Turkey, will attend the meeting. (different)

B. Words with Different Meanings

Match the word in bold with its definition.

1 UNICEF is a **charity** that gives medicine and educational funds to children in need. ______
The man is full of **charity**. He has a very good heart. ______
Definition: ⓐ *n.* an organization that helps people ⓑ *n.* compassion and good will

2 We all love your poem and think it has a lot of **worth**. ______
Several dollars' **worth** of beef should feed the whole family for a day. ______
Definition: ⓐ *n.* the value of something in money ⓑ *n.* value or importance

3 We **raised** $5,000 to buy toys for poor children. ______
The government is **raising** taxes to pay for the war. ______
Definition: ⓐ *v.* to increase ⓑ *v.* to collect money for a cause

C. Multiple Choice

Circle the correct answers.

1. Why does Dump & Run collect used items from college students?
   a. to recycle the items
   b. to resell them for charity
   c. to do a class project
   d. to fix any items that are broken

2. How does Tom Cody raise donations using adDonations.com?
   a. He simply asks people for money.
   b. He posts videos of people in need online.
   c. He sells advertising space.
   d. He organizes a community event.

3. What is collected at the AXE Undie Run Challenge?
   a. clothing
   b. food
   c. medicine
   d. money

4. How do students raise money at THON?
   a. The students collect money door to door.
   b. The students do community service.
   c. They sell secondhand clothing.
   d. The students dance all night.

UNIT 12

Your Career Starts Now

These days, young people are applying for positior interns while they're still students. You usually don't r any money in an internship, but the experience you and the people you meet often make it worthwhile.

Words & Expressions

Task I *Listen and fill in the blanks in the column.* Track 46

qualified	employer	available	sociable
internship	communication	employment	advice

Tuesday, February 15th

Career Doctor — What Employers Want

Dear Career Doctor,

I'm still in university, but my dad says it's sensible to start looking for work now. What do you think?

M

Dear M,

It's never too early to look for ❶ ____________. My ❷ ____________ is to start early. Then you can see what's ❸ ____________ while you're still at school. A summer ❹ ____________ will increase your chances of finding a good job when you graduate. Before you go for an interview, research the potential ❺ ____________ and the position. There will be many ❻ ____________ people, so focus on your "soft skills," like problem solving and working as part of a team. Be enthusiastic and remember that ❼ ____________ is number one. Employers don't just want great students; they want people who are ❽ ____________ and flexible too!

The Career Doctor

Task II *Write the word from **Task I** next to its matching definition or synonym.*

1. reasonable: ____________	2. work: ____________	3. possible: ____________
4. accessible: ____________	5. a short-term job: ____________	6. interested and willing: ____________
7. friendly: ____________	8. a job, post: ____________	9. having skills: ____________

Task III *Use the words from **Task II** to complete the sentences.*

1. Ray is a very ____________ guy. He has lots of friends.
2. If you're not ____________, you won't get the job.
3. We had the lowest ____________ rate last year.
4. She's ____________ not to spend all her money on clothes.
5. To win, the team needs to be more ____________.
6. A(n) ____________ problem is that we might not have enough money.

Listen Up

*Listen and check **True** or **False**.* Track 47

	True	False
1. The speaker is a university student.	☐	☐
2. He thinks that the way people act is important.	☐	☐
3. You have to find out what kind of job suits you first.	☐	☐
4. You don't need to be qualified to get the job.	☐	☐
5. When going for a job, you should think about the job and your skills.	☐	☐

Language Tip

*Fill in the chart with **employ**, **employee**, **employer**, and **employment**.*

	(*n.*) one who pays people to work		(*n.*) one who is paid to work
	(*v.*) to pay someone to work for you		(*n.*) a job

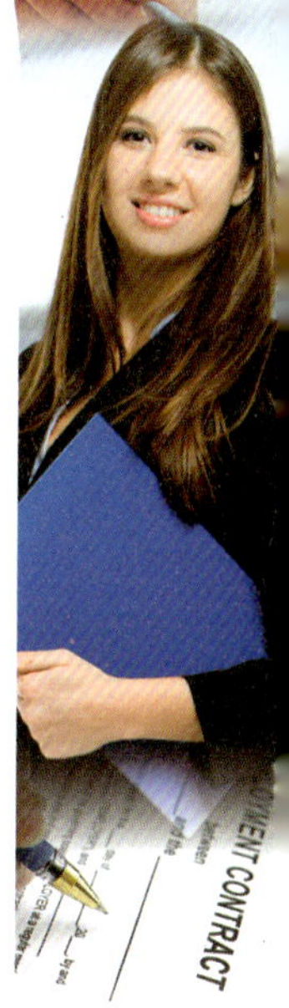

Use the correct form of the words above to complete the sentences.

1. Jacob is the newest ______________ in our office. He's been working here for three months.
2. The company is pretty big. It ______________ over 500 people.
3. Tessa is bored with her job, so she's looking for new ______________.
4. The factory is the biggest ______________ in the town.

Class Interview

Talk to your partner. Which of these do you need for a good workplace?

	Not Needed	Useful	Essential
1. Shared responsibility			
2. An employer with a good attitude			
3. The chance to demonstrate your skills			
4. Strong management			
5. Workers who have talent			
6. Staff with good qualifications			
7. Rewards for great work			

Share your partner's opinions with the class using the expressions below.

working as a team	a positive boss	the opportunity to show what you can do
good leadership	people with natural abilities	satisfying work

My partner thinks that ______________________ is / are the most important thing in a company.

Conversation

The Job Fair

Fill in the blanks with the word choices given. Then listen to check your answers. Track 48

internship	essential	expert	demonstrating	attitude

Matt talks to Trey outside the classroom.

Matt: Did you hear about the career fair today? Do you want to go check it out?

Trey: Um, I'm not sure. I've got to study to pass this test.

Matt: What are you worrying for? You have enough time to do both.

Trey: What's going on at the fair anyway?

Matt: Employers will be there, obviously. Someone will give a speech on communication too. I'm going there to look for a(n) **1.** __________.

Trey: It's likely that your dad will be there to speak. He's a career **2.** __________, right?

Matt: A career consultant, yeah. He knows employment from A to Z. He's always advising me to study and telling me that qualifications are **3.** __________.

Trey: You're lucky that jobs are his subject. I'll have a hard time when I need to find work. I'm too lazy to get a job!

Matt: There's no need to worry. You're sociable, and you've got the talent and the right **4.** __________. There's a good chance you'll find a job straight after graduation.

Trey: Well, thanks, but I'm not qualified yet! Let's go see what's available.

Matt: I'm going to start **5.** __________ leadership right now. Follow me!

Trey: I'm right behind you!

A. Meanings in Context

Choose the meaning of the sentence in the conversation.

1. What's going on at the fair anyway? **a.** Will the fair last a long time? **b.** What's happening there?	**2.** He knows employment from A to Z. **a.** He can spell the word *employment*. **b.** He knows a lot about it.
3. I'll have a hard time when I need to find work. **a.** I think looking for work is exciting. **b.** Looking for a job will be very difficult for me.	**4.** There's a good chance you'll find a job straight after graduation. **a.** You'll probably find a job soon. **b.** You'll have opportunities if you are honest.

B. Words with Different Meanings

Match the word in bold with its definition.

1. Water is **essential** to life on earth. ______

   When you're mountain climbing, a good bag is an **essential**. ______

   Definition: ⓐ *adj.* important or needed ⓑ *n.* something basic or necessary

2. There are still tickets **available** for the play. ______

   Mr. Thompson isn't **available** at the moment. He's in a meeting. ______

   Definition: ⓐ *adj.* can be bought or gotten ⓑ *adj.* not busy

3. You need to **demonstrate** confidence when you teach a class. ______

   Elaine will now **demonstrate** the new software for us. ______

   Definition: ⓐ *v.* to show how to do or use something ⓑ *v.* to show an ability or feeling

C. Expressions

Giving Encouragement

What are you worrying for?	You'll be fine. / It'll be fine.
There's no need to worry.	Don't worry.
It isn't as bad as all that.	There's nothing to worry about.

Create some dialogues using the ideas below.

Student A	have lost the keys	haven't gotten any money	didn't bring the book
Student B	roommate has the keys	can lend you some	you can share mine

A: I'm in big trouble! I've lost my keys, and I can't get into my house.

B: Don't worry. It isn't as bad as all that. Your roommate has the keys, right? You can wait at my house.

Grammar

Infinitives

Infinitives with *Too* and *Enough*

Sentence Pattern	Example
too much / many (+ Noun) + to Verb too + Adjective + to Verb	I have too much homework to do. I'm too lazy to get a job!
enough (+ Noun) + to Verb Adjective + enough + to Verb	You have enough time to do both. They're old enough to know better.

Infinitive Commands

An **infinitive** is often used with command verbs. These include **advise**, **require**, **ask**, and **order**. The meaning is the same as using a that clause. The verb in the clause must take the base form.

Command with *Infinitive*	Command with *That Clause*
He's always advising me to study.	He's always advising that I study.
They require the student to pass the exam.	They require that the student pass the exam.
The teacher asked her to stand.	The teacher asked that she stand.
The boss ordered him to work harder.	The boss ordered that he work harder.

Infinitives of Purpose

Form	Example
Subject + Verb + in order to Verb	I'm going to the fair in order to look for an internship.
Subject + Verb + to Verb	I'm going to the fair to look for an internship.
In order to Verb, Subject + Verb	In order to look for an internship, I'm going to the fair.
To Verb, Subject + Verb	To look for an internship, I'm going to the fair.

Usage Note

We use **to Verb** or **for + Verb + -ing** to talk about what things are used for. For a reason that one does something, only use **an infinitive**.

For Example:

I use a spoon **to eat / for eating soup**.
I went to the restaurant **to eat dinner**.

A. Match

Match the two parts.

1.	Harry turned off his phone	to stay where he was.
2.	I'm not small enough	to wait for the tickets.
3.	We stopped in the shade	to make herself feel better.
4.	Gina took some medicine	to attend the meeting.
5.	Jeremy joined the line	to cool down.
6.	The college asked me	to go to bed.
7.	It's too early	in order to stop it from ringing.
8.	Instead of moving, I advised him	to get through the hole.

B. Fill in the Blanks

Use the verbs below to complete the sentences.

to stay	to have	to repair	to read
to bring	to be	to make	to pick

1. I'm too young ______________ gray hair.
2. The roof of the house is too old ______________.
3. Cathy wore high heels ______________ herself look taller.
4. I'm not strong enough ______________ up the luggage.
5. Jimmy put on his coat in order ______________ warm.
6. The professor ordered Eva ______________ on time for class.
7. My vision isn't good enough ______________ the text.
8. The new law requires you ______________ your ID with you.

C. Correct the Mistakes

Fix the errors in the passage.

When I was 14, I was too young ~~driving~~ to drive. I always rode my bike order to get to school. My brother, Dennis, was too old enough to get a license, but he didn't have any money for a car. My father advised us that get part-time jobs. It wasn't easy for us to earns the money, but at the end of a year we had enough buy a secondhand car. After that, we drove to the lake where nobody could tell us what do. It was a great way spend time, and we still go fishing there sometimes. I wish we still had time to go every weekend though.

Reading

Before You Read

Discuss the following questions with a partner:

1. Do you know about any interesting work customs in other parts of the world?
2. Is your country's work culture relaxed or formal?

Work Cultures of the World

Track 49

As our world becomes more globalized, international business is on the rise. Although business practices can differ within an individual country, it is important to have a sense of acceptable behavior in other cultures. This will guarantee better communication and a more pleasant work experience.

Some countries are known for having a laid back approach to work. In France, a law was passed in 2000 which reduced many employees' schedules to 35 hours per week. France also has 11 national holidays, so employees enjoy more frequent time off. Likewise, Spain's businesses have a very flexible mentality. Most companies in Spain allow for a 2-hour "siesta" in the middle of the work day. Many Spanish employees take this opportunity to go home, rest, and spend time with their families.

In other countries, work styles can be considered more serious but also very efficient. For example, Japan is known for its long work hours and more serious attitude. Japanese workers demonstrate this seriousness with their unique listening style. They may close their eyes when they are trying to respectfully focus on what someone is saying. Seriousness and respect are important in the Japanese culture, especially when it involves elders in the work setting.

While German employees may not work long hours like the Japanese, their very formal attitude allows them to complete tasks in a timely manner. They don't engage in much small talk and instead consider direct and blunt communication to be most effective. Germans find it very important to be punctual. You would likely receive criticism if you arrived late to a meeting in Germany.

As you enter the work force and interact with people from all over the world, it's important to know more about their cultures. A little bit of cultural awareness can add much to your work experience.

A. Synonyms

Match the word in bold with its synonym.

differ •	• cooperate
acceptable •	• manner
attitude •	• effective
efficient •	• suitable
respect •	• blame
complete •	• admiration
criticism •	• vary
interact •	• finish

B. Word Definitions

Use the clues to fill in the blanks with the word choices given.

globalized	behavior	frequent	guarantee	laid back	flexible	blunt	punctual

1. My sister is very ______________. She always says what's on her mind. (straightforward)
2. As Korea becomes more ______________, the need for global communication skills increases. (international)
3. The job requires ______________ business trips abroad. (numerous)
4. Can you ______________ that this car won't break down after a week? (promise)
5. My friends call me a very ______________ person since I'm always on time. (prompt)
6. I'm calling to see how ______________ your schedule is today. (adaptable)
7. Be careful of your ______________ on a formal occasion. (manners)
8. Everyone here has a really ______________ attitude. (relaxed)

C. Multiple Choice

Circle the correct answers.

1. Work practices in Spain and France are ______________.
   a. extremely different. One culture is more serious than the other
   b. similar because both cultures are considered laid-back
   c. neither casual nor formal
   d. very efficient and intense

2. To focus on listening, Japanese workers might ______________.
   a. close their eyes
   b. cover their mouths
   c. cross their arms
   d. nod their heads

3. Which of the following is important to Japanese people?
   a. respecting their elders in the work setting
   b. honestly criticizing lazy coworkers
   c. waiting for the other person to nod
   d. putting emphasis on taking vacations

4. How do Germans communicate?
   a. They speak politely and rarely criticize.
   b. They try to speak in a formal way.
   c. They speak in a very direct way.
   d. They only pay attention to body language.

Writing

STUDENT BOOK 3

Writing

Task I *Read the ad below. Underline the qualities that Jenna is looking for in a roommate.*

Need a Responsible Roommate

I'm a 20-year-old female history student at UCLA. I'm looking for a tidy and friendly roommate to share a two-bedroom apartment near the university. The apartment has furniture, Internet, and cable TV. We will share a bathroom and a living room. The available bedroom is large. The rent is $250 a month. The perfect roommate would also be a student. I have a small dog, so you have to like dogs. I also can't take any other pets. If you are a smoker, you MUST smoke on the balcony. I get along well with creative and knowledgeable people. I'm pretty talkative and would be happy to live with a similar person.

Please send me an e-mail (jennabusybee@ucla.edu) and tell me about yourself. I would like to hear about your studies, personality, and why you would make a good roommate.

Jenna

Task II *Write an e-mail to Jenna. Tell her about yourself. The phrases below may help.*

pay the rent on time	clean up after myself all the time	know a lot of things
like to have a good conversation	play the piano and draw	*your own description*

Hi Jenna,

My name is ____________________. I'm responding to your ad looking for a roommate.

____

____

____

____

____

____

____

I think we would make good roommates. When would be the best time to see the room?

Best,

____

Writing

Task I *Your friend is coming to visit. He has questions about shopping. Finish the e-mail using the hints.*

From:

Hello!

I can't wait to see you next month. I have a few questions about your country.

______________________________ (go shopping, visit).

______________________________ (electronics, clothes, books).

______________________________ (recommend)?

______________________________ (cheapest places)?

______________________________ (reliable places)?

______________________________ (sales, this time of year)?

______________________________ (stores, crowded)?

Any advice would help me a lot.

Thanks!

Leo

Task II *Write a reply letter using some of the words and phrases below.*

bargains	suggest	night markets	selection	price	watch out for
not certain	convenient	products	sales	discounts	crowded

From:

Dear Leo,

I'm very happy that you are coming to visit me. ______________________________

____

____

____

____

____

I look forward to seeing you.

Regards,

Bruce

Writing

Task I *You are a trainer. Read the ad and think about how you can help Dan. Write some notes on the right.*

WANTED: Personal Trainer

I'm looking for someone to help me lose weight. I also want to get back in shape again. I'm so busy that I can't make time for exercise. I haven't exercised in a few years, and I'm really packing on the pounds. I need somebody to motivate me. Do you have any advice? The job is part-time, three days a week. You can contact me by e-mail at dan@sterlingarcher.com. I'm looking forward to hearing from you!

Dan

Why are you the best trainer?

____

____

How will you change his diet and exercise?

____

____

Questions to ask him (time / diet / work):

____

____

____

Task II *Reply to Dan's ad. Include some of the words and phrases below.*

concentrate on nutrition	go on a diet	low in fat	small portions
current weight	get daily exercise	work out at home	accompany
take a run in the park	on average	other health problems	

Hi Dan,

I'm ______________, and I've been a personal trainer for ______________. I saw your ad, and I think I can help you. ______________________________

____

____

____

____

____

I hope this helps. When would you like to start?

Yours,

____

Writing

Task I *You work for a newspaper advice column. Read the following letter and write some notes.*

Dear Dr. K.,

I really like my boyfriend, and he feels the same way about me. We've been going out for about a year, and we've never argued. The problem is that he is moving to Australia for a year, and I can't go with him. I'm worried about it. I'm very busy with college, and I don't have enough money or time to go visit him. We have a great time when we're together on the weekends, but we don't talk too much during the week. How will it work if we never see each other? Will we be faithful to each other? Should we just split up?

Yours,

Worried Girl

Reasons to Stay Together	Reasons to Split Up

Task II *Write a reply using some of the words and phrases below and tag questions.*

cheat on	argument	conflict	relationship	get along as friends
work out	communicate	break up	on the other hand	are willing to
keep in touch				

Dear Worried Girl,

It's quite difficult for both of you, isn't it? ______________________

____

____

____

____

____

Remember, you'll have to work hard at it. Good luck!

Yours,

Dr. K.

Writing

Task I *Read the flyer below. Fill in the blanks with appropriate adjectives to convince more people to come.*

Event: Chinese New Year Parade

Date and Time: February 19th, 5:00 – 8:00 p.m.

Place: San Francisco

Activities and Sights: costumes, firecrackers, martial arts

REUTERS / Stephen Lam

Come to the biggest Asian festival outside of Asia: the annual San Francisco Chinese New Year celebration! Thousands of people wear ______________ costumes and walk in the streets of San Francisco. There are many ______________ musicians, dancers, and martial arts performers. The most ______________ performer of the festival is Gum Lung, the Golden Dragon of Chinatown. The Golden Dragon walks at the end of the parade. It takes 100 people to carry it. More than a million people come to see and take part in this ______________ festival every year. This is a(n)______________ event that should not be missed!

Task II *Finish the flyer using the information given. The words and phrases below may help you.*

take place	lanterns	on display	well-known artists	amazing
designs	terrific	fun activities	traditional foods	be released
extraordinary				

Event: Lantern Festival Celebration

Date and Time: February 17th – 19th, 2:00 – 9:00 p.m.

Place: Pingxi town center

Activities: music, art displays
(2,000 free sky lanterns will be given out.)

Come to the celebration of the Lantern Festival at Pingxi!

____

____

____

____

____

Task I *Your cousin is opening an art gallery in London and has written to you. Read the letter and make some notes.*

Hello from London!

It's great to be doing this finally. The gallery is nearly finished, and I'm putting some art in it now. Most of my art is from Europe, and I think it's a little boring to only have European art. I'm writing to ask you if you have any ideas about Asian art. Maybe one of your friends is an artist, or you know about a famous artist. If so, tell me about his or her art and send me a picture or two.

Best,

Philip

Friend's / artist's name: ____________________ Type of art: ____________________

How is it different from European art?

____

Describe one of his / her pieces.

____

Task II *Reply to your cousin using some of the words and phrases below.*

creative	Eastern	traditional	landscape	photography
oil on canvas	sculpture	has a gift for	masterpiece	abstract
impressed by				

Dear Philip,

It's great to hear from you! ____________________

____

____

____

____

I'm sending you a photo of __________. You're welcome to take a look and decide.

Regards,

____

Writing

Task I *Arrange the types of television shows from 1 (your favorite) to 8 (your least favorite). Then choose the statements you agree with.*

	1 - 8
current affairs	
soap opera	
documentary	
reality	
comedy	
sports	
drama	
game show	

		☑ / ☒
TV is for	education.	
	entertainment.	
	both.	

	☑ / ☒
I watch a lot of television.	
I prefer to watch alone.	
I watch television online.	
I think kids shouldn't watch so much.	

Task II *Write a passage about your television habits. Use some of the words and phrases below. Include two examples of the* ***present perfect continuous****.*

sitcoms	put my feet up	viewer	commercials	reality shows
can't stand	live television	game shows	characters	newscasters

For Example:

My name is Jane, and I watch a lot of television. I like to watch things online as well. Then you can watch whole seasons. I've been doing that for a year or so …

My name is ________________________________

Writing

Task I *Read the two flyers below. Decide which concert you would like to go to and answer the questions.*

Name: **Damien Rice** ☐	Name: **The White Stripes** ☐
Type: **Singer / songwriter**	Type: **Rock**
Date: **July 14th**	Date: **July 25th**
Location: **Shibuya Plug** (600 people)	Location: **The O2 Arena** (20,000 people)
Instruments: **Guitar, vocals**	Instruments: **Electric guitar, drums, vocals, piano**

1. What's your favorite type of music? ______________________
2. Do you prefer small concerts or big ones? ______________________
3. What instrument(s) do you like / play? ______________________
4. Would you like to be a famous musician? ______________________

Task II *Write about your experiences with music. Talk about your favorite music, concerts, and musicians. Use some of the words and phrases below.*

musicians	unknown	household name	piano	guitar
keyboard	drums	live	sold out	amazing
outstanding	inspired	influenced	original	stars

My favorite ____

Writing

Task I *An American friend of yours wants to study abroad. She has never left the country before. Fill in the blanks in the e-mail she wrote you.*

Hi!

I'm thinking about going to Taiwan to study Chinese. I __________ (worried, leaving) though. This would be my first time. Where __________ __________ (information, Taiwan)? How do I __________ __________ (student visa)? It would __________ __________ (fun, experience, culture), but I'm __________ (concerned, language). What is __________ (best school)? I will be __________ (less scared, assistance).

Thank you so much!

Allie

Task II *Write a reply to Allie. Answer her questions and tell her about Taiwan. Use some of the words and phrases below.*

language barrier	look online	apply for	make arrangements	semester
make an effort	homesick	don't be afraid of	be a breeze	process
surroundings	independence	assistance		

Hey Allie!

I'm glad to hear that you might be coming! __________

____

____

____

____

____

____

See you soon!

____

Writing

Task I *Fill in the blanks in the timeline and answer the questions.*

home computer	radio	touch screen phone	lightbulb	Internet	television

1879 ____________ 1895 ____________ 1923 ____________ 1969 ____________ 1975 ____________ 1992 ____________

1. What do you think is the greatest invention of all time?

____

2. What do we use it for?

____

3. How has it changed our lives?

____

Task II *Research an invention on the Internet and write a paragraph about it. Include vocabulary from below.*

handy	people say	cost an arm and a leg	high-tech	practical
high-quality	worth it	development	quality	convenience
state-of-the-art	technology	ahead of the times		

My favorite invention is ______________________________

Writing

Task I *A friend of yours is working in Germany. Read her e-mail and fill in the blanks.*

suspended	inform	dumped	relationship	problem

Hello! Long time no see!

I've wanted to write to you for a while, but things are pretty busy here. My new job is great. I work late a lot, but the money is good. The only ❶ ____________ is the supervisor. He's been seeing one of the other workers here. At first, everything was OK, but then she decided to end the ❷ ____________. He got very angry and ❸ ____________ her from work. He said her work was poor, but everyone knows it was because she ❹ ____________ him. I don't know what to do. She's my friend. Should I talk to him, ❺ ____________ his boss, or just keep quiet?

Need some advice!

Clara

Task II *Reply to Clara's letter. Talk about her job and give her some advice. Use some of the words and phrases below.*

tired out	suspended	breaking up with	moral	behavior
take the risk	inform	otherwise	ruin	reputation
evidence	rumors	get in trouble	see red	mess with

Hello Clara!

I'm so happy that you finally wrote! ____

____

____

____

____

____

I hope it works out. Good luck!

Regards,

____

Writing

Task I *Match the expressions and underline the formal ones.*

1. Yours sincerely,	position
2. Dear Sir or Madam,	I am writing to inquire about …
3. job	I would be grateful if …
4. I look forward to hearing from you.	Talk to you later.
5. Tell me about …	Hope to talk to you soon.
6. It would be super if …	Hi!

Task II *You are writing a cover letter for a job. Imagine a good job and write down what experience you have.*

Position: ______________

Employer: ______________

Experience: ______________________________

Write your letter using the formal phrases above and some of the vocabulary below.

position	employer	skills	take responsibility	sociable
attitude	experience	internship	degree	qualified
graduation	interview	demonstrate	résumé	

NOTES

NOTES

NOTES